Schools as
PROFESSIONAL
LEARNING
Communities

Schools as PROFESSIONAL LEARNING Communities

Collaborative Activities and Strategies for Professional Development

Sylvia M. Roberts
Eunice Z. Pruitt

Foreword by Susan Sullivan

CORWIN PRESS, INC.
A Sage Publications Company
Thousand Oaks, California

For information:

Corwin Press, Inc.
A Sage Publications Company
2455 Teller Road
Thousand Oaks, California 91320
www.corwinpress.com

Sage Publications Ltd.
6 Bonhill Street
London EC2A 4PU
United Kingdom

Sage Publications India Pvt. Ltd.
B-42, Panchsheel Enclave
Post Box 4109
New Delhi 110 017 India

Printed in the United States of America

Library of Congress Cataloging-in-Publication Data

Roberts, Sylvia M. (Sylvia Mae), 1937-
Schools as professional learning communities : collaborative activities and strategies for professional development / Sylvia M. Roberts, Eunice Z. Pruitt.
     p. cm.
Includes bibliographical references and index.
ISBN 0-7619-4581-4 (Cloth)—ISBN 0-7619-4582-2 (Paper)
   1. Group work in education—United States. 2. Activity programs in education—United States. 3. Teachers-In-service training—United States. I. Pruitt, Eunice Z. (Eunice Zita) II. Title.
LB1032.R59 2003
371.14′8—dc21

                                                2003008013

This book is printed on acid-free paper.

             05   06   07   7   6   5   4   3

Acquisitions Editor:	Rachel Livsey
Editorial Assistant:	Phyllis Cappello
Production Editor:	Julia Parnell
Typesetter:	C&M Digitals (P) Ltd.
Proofreader:	Colleen Brennan
Indexer:	Teri Greenberg
Cover Designer:	Tracy E. Miller
Production Artist:	Lisa Miller

Contents

Foreword

Every year, my colleagues who teach educational administration and provide support for practicing leaders peruse the literature seeking appropriate texts for our administrative candidates and leaders. And every year we come up with a group of books, each of which fulfills one facet of the theory and practice issues we would like addressed. Some books are primarily theoretical and frustrate practitioners who need to link theory and practice as they learn and subsequently implement. Others are purely practical and do not provide a conceptual framework for their recipes for administrative success. Many textbooks offer a step-by-step procedural guide for administrators, despite the research evidence that one size does not fit all. Texts that are primarily collections of case studies contain stories and scenarios that may or may not be applicable or useful to the reader, particularly because studies about others do not usually influence the learner's "theory-in-use," that is, actual practice.

Schools as Professional Learning Communities is the exceptional book that neither limits itself to one theoretical focus nor tries to offer a how-to script. What does it accomplish and how does it reach its goal?

The first chapter introduces a conceptual framework that undergirds the rest of the book. Roberts and Pruitt pull together many of the central concepts and theoretical architects of the learning community and use their ideas to answer key questions about the learning community. The first chapter also sets the format for the rest of the book. The questions posed at the beginning of the chapter frame the discussion. The authors respond with a clear and concise description of the characteristics of the learning community. The subsequent chapters explore the characteristics of the school structures that emanate from this conceptual framework and offer strategies, tips, and processes for their development.

Each chapter focuses on at least one concept of the learning community and then offers multiple strategies and activities upon which the community-building process can be based. Alternative suggestions and a choice of resources to foster development of each learning characteristic allow the designated or potential leader to make adaptations to his or her specific site. Brief supporting case studies and scenarios based on the authors' extensive professional experiences as leaders and facilitators help authenticate the ideas and clarify the suggested activities. Tips for Leaders and sample implementation and feedback forms permit the leader pressed for time to operationalize the strategies quickly. The ongoing references to Websites and to the related literature expand the reader's options for reflection and implementation. These references make the text more user and reader friendly. And every chapter concludes with suggestions for reflection and practice that can also help get the change process off the ground.

The book's readability is essential for the overburdened leader, teacher-leader, and the prospective administrators who will need to convey the newly learned ideas and strategies to their colleagues and staff. Educational jargon has been by and large eliminated. The few remaining necessary words that underlie concepts are defined and supported by examples. The questions at the beginning of each chapter pique the reader's interest and then serve as a guide throughout the chapter.

The tone also sustains interest. It is conversational, accessible, friendly, and collegial. One has the feeling that Roberts and Pruitt are in conversation with each other and the readers. The authors' combined knowledge and vast personal experiences with each characteristic of the learning community give life to the examples, scenarios, and suggestions. The tone has another quality: respect for the educator. For example, the inclusion of references to key books and Websites presumes the professionalism of the reader. The writers expect that the readers will supplement their knowledge and skills as needed through the recommended resources.

This assumption of professionalism forms part of one of the most admirable features of the text: the modeling of the creation of a learning community. First, the book's orientation toward leadership is inclusive. All staff members in a school can readily understand *Schools as Professional Learning Communities* and can choose which concepts or characteristics they would like to encourage at their site, thereby engaging in the establishment of their learning community. The book's readability, fostering of reflection, rich spectrum of approaches for building a learning community, and myriad points of departure for promoting each characteristic exemplify how the readers themselves can proceed. Thus, in the writing of this rich, comprehensive, and at the same time accessible book, Roberts and Pruitt set the stage for the creation of communities of learners.

—Susan Sullivan

Preface

This book is about strategies for providing learning opportunities for teachers that lead to the building of community in schools. The literature on school reform currently reflects a shift from the paradigm of schools as organizations to schools as learning communities. This change essentially represents a new way in which to view schools and the relationships among staff members in schools. One purpose of this book is to provide those who wear the mantle of leadership in the new paradigm with the knowledge and skills they need to work effectively with teachers, parents, administrators, students, and the community at large.

It is our belief (a) that the learning community paradigm is central to the development of an improved pedagogy, and (b) that improved teaching, learning, and educational outcomes for students can be achieved when teachers come together to collaboratively search for and resolve the problems of practice in their schools. With these beliefs as a framework, the pivotal ideas that informed the development of this text, which have been borne out in the literature, are as follows:

1. Although principals may lead the transformation process, leadership can come from teachers, if they are provided with opportunities to assume meaningful leadership roles in the school improvement process.

2. Providing high-quality collaborative learning opportunities for teachers can result in improved learning opportunities for students (Lambert, 1998).

3. Meaningful and continuous conversation among teachers about their beliefs, their teaching, their learning, and what they have learned about teaching is necessary for teachers to develop into a community of learners and leaders (Kruse, Louis, & Bryk, 1995).

4. Restructuring cannot result simply from fixing, adding, or subtracting new parts to a school's programs. Real change requires

that teachers have opportunities to continually reexamine their educational beliefs and the assumptions that guide their behavior (Senge et al., 2000).

In our work, we have seen many schools where there are dedicated leaders and teachers who have noble intentions but where movement toward effective classroom practice among teachers has been repeatedly stymied by the top-down implementation of the latest well-marketed model of school reform. At the same time, we have found that instructional improvement is most likely when teachers and supervisors are afforded structured learning opportunities and when they take collective responsibility for using their newly acquired knowledge to accomplish shared educational goals.

Although this book is not primarily about the research base that undergirds the efficacy of the learning communities paradigm, our work has been influenced by the thinking and research of a number of prominent writers in the area of learning communities, school restructuring, change processes, and group processes. Linda Lambert's groundbreaking work (Lambert, 1998; Lambert et al., 1995) on constructivist leadership provides the basis for our thinking about leadership in the learning community. The work of Louis and Kruse (1995) offers clear-cut evidence of the connection between collaborative school structures and the building of professional community. Sergiovanni's (2001) writing continually stimulates our thinking about the principalship and the building of community.

The specific strategies and ideas that we have set out to share with our readers have been gleaned from the wide-ranging research base, from literature, and from in-depth conversations with teachers and supervisors in a variety of contexts. They have been refined in extensive staff development activities that we have conducted and observed while assisting schools and leaders of schools in their improvement efforts.

Optimistically, we set out to write a book that contained elements that were friendly and useful, first for practitioners who are charged with guiding the transformation of their schools into learning communities, and second for higher education faculty who face a mandate to provide more relevant instruction in teacher and administrator preparation programs. Additionally, we had in mind the needs of the increasing number of study groups, learning circles, and school leadership teams that we see proliferating in the many schools that we visit. To serve these audiences, we have focused on the operational level of learning community schools. The strategies, tips, and activities presented are all associated with job-embedded learning—learning that addresses the immediate issues faced by the teachers in their classrooms; that targets the work that teachers, supervisors, and other school personnel perform in their day-to-day work lives; and that ultimately leads to the assumption of a leadership role by all members of the school community.

ORGANIZATION OF THE BOOK AND CHAPTER OVERVIEWS

The book is divided into nine chapters. The format for each chapter is basically the same. Each chapter opens with a preview and a set of key questions that focus the reader's attention on the knowledge, strategies, and leadership behaviors that are addressed in the chapter. As we crafted the text, we were ever-mindful of the need to articulate the importance for those in formal leadership positions to continually seek ways of shaping learning opportunities for teachers and other educators so that they might effectively share the leadership role in their schools.

Learning activities, related case studies, tips for leaders, and online information are provided to facilitate the implementation of the strategies discussed in each chapter. The online information serves to illustrate and reinforce understanding of the topics developed in the text, to lead the reader to other resources on the topic, and/or to provide opportunities for practicing the strategies.

Chapter 1 provides an overview of the underlying research on, rationale for, and theoretical underpinnings of the learning community paradigm, and includes an in-depth discussion of the characteristics of a learning community. This chapter forms the foundation on which subsequent chapters are developed.

In Chapter 2, which has leadership as its focus, we apply Linda Lambert's model of constructivist leadership to the development of a learning community. The role of the principal and practical strategies and tips for fulfilling the role are presented. The importance and the relationship of the concepts of shared leadership and shared vision and detailed steps for developing a shared vision statement are central ideas in this chapter. This chapter also introduces the basic communication skills, change processes, and strategies necessary for effectively providing leadership in a learning community.

Chapter 3 examines principles, standards, and strategies for effective professional development, as well as ways of evaluating the staff development program. The needs of the staff as adult learners are highlighted.

Chapter 4 explores aspects of working in groups, including team processes, dealing with conflict, group decision making and problem solving, and conducting meetings. Teamwork is essential to a community of learners, and it is enhanced by a knowledge of group processes and dynamics.

The importance of the use of study groups as a strategy for building a learning community is explored in Chapter 5. The material is presented in a user-friendly way that provides practical strategies, tips, and resources needed to initiate study groups in their schools. The role of principals and supervisors in implementing study groups is explored, and case studies to clarify the process are provided.

Chapter 6 presents information on how to afford learning opportunities for teachers through the process of classroom observation. In this chapter, classroom observation is presented in a broader context than the conventional approach to this topic. Classroom observation in the learning community is associated with and includes all strategies that permit educators to observe instructional activities, events, or resources in one another's classroom with a view toward the improvement of instruction.

Chapter 7 deals with other collaborative ways of improving instruction in learning communities. It examines mentoring, collaborative assessment of student work, and other cooperative approaches for improving instruction.

Chapter 8 examines professional portfolios as another learning opportunity. It offers tips for developing professional portfolios, using them at various career stages, and evaluating them.

Chapter 9 discusses ways of sustaining the learning community. It examines school culture and the importance of celebrating success. It also explores strategies for maintaining the focus on a school's mission and vision and strengthening shared leadership.

HOW TO USE THIS BOOK

Our goal in writing this book was to provide educators with the practical knowledge and field-based strategies that would empower them to guide teachers, parents, students, and other stakeholders in transforming their schools into learning communities. Each chapter can be read independently, but we strongly suggest that a reading of the first three chapters prior to reading other chapters will provide the foundation for a deeper understanding of the rationale behind the strategies provided throughout the book. The activities provided throughout and at the end of almost every chapter are appropriate for use by study groups or school leadership teams as they seek to build their learning communities.

The sequence of topics as presented in this book should not be considered as step-by-step guidelines for the building of a learning community. We did not intend to provide a cookbook for solving the problems that schools undergoing change currently face, nor do we believe that such an approach toward building learning communities is feasible or logically defensible. Selection of strategies for use at a given school site should be based on the needs, readiness level, and culture of that school.

The vignettes about the Menlo school, which are to be found throughout the book, are fictitious, but they represent a compilation of our experiences over many years of working with school districts. The names of the people working in the Menlo schools are also fictional. Other schools and people mentioned by name are real.

The Websites selected for inclusion in the text, which give examples of the nature of the resources available on the Web, were current at the time of publication. Given the ever-increasing volume of relevant resources, readers are encouraged to supplement these sites by conducting their own searches of the World Wide Web.

Acknowledgments

A debt of gratitude is owed to the many dedicated teachers, administrators, supervisors, and other school district personnel with whom we have worked and from whom we have learned much about the importance of building community and the process of school reform.

We are grateful to our supportive families and friends for putting up with us as we used so much of our time to reflect on and complete this book.

We thank Rachel Livsey, acquisitions editor at Corwin Press, her editorial assistant, Phyllis Cappello, and Stacey Shimizu, our copy editor, for their professionalism and responsiveness as we worked to complete the manuscript. Our appreciation is also offered to the reviewers whose useful comments served to validate and refine our work.

Finally, we must thank one another. We have both benefited in meaningful ways from the discussions, teaching, research, and writing activities that we have collaborated on over the past 10 years. We have learned even more about schooling as we struggled to complete this manuscript in the face of the competing priorities of our professional and personal lives.

The contributions of the following reviewers are gratefully acknowledged:

Steve Hutton
Educator
Kentucky Department of Education
Villa Hills, KY

Mary Ann Sweet
School Counselor
Tomball Elementary
Tomball, TX

Jennifer York-Barr
Associate Professor and Coordinator
University of Minnesota
Minneapolis, MN

Michelle Collay, PhD
School Coach
Bay Area Coalition of Equitable Schools
Oakland, CA

Karen Coblentz
Principal
Dassel Elementary
Dassel, MN

David Schumaker
Superintendent
Mountain Valley Unified School District
Hayfork, CA

Walter Enloe
Associate Professor
Hamline University
St. Paul, MN

Peter Grande
Director of Professional Development
Rose Tree Media School District
Media, PA

Darlene A. Merry
Associate Superintendent
Office of Staff Development
Montgomery County Public Schools
Rockville, MD

The cooperation of the following principals is greatly appreciated:

Peter McFarlane
Hugo Newman College
   Preparatory School
Newyork, NY

Gloria Williams
Evergreen School
Plainfield, NJ

To my family—Janet, Harriet, William, Pam, and Gary
Sylvia Roberts

To my husband, Henry, my children, grandchildren, and family
Eunice Zita Pruitt

About the Authors

Sylvia Roberts is a member of the faculty and the head of the Programs in Educational Administration and Supervision at the City College of New York. She teaches graduate coursework in educational administration and supervision. Her special areas of focus are leadership, curriculum development and supervision, content research in educational administration, and the integration of technology into administrator preparation programs.

Dr. Roberts completed her PhD in educational administration at New York University.

During her tenure at the New Jersey State Department of Education, she was responsible for the statewide oversight and management of Compensatory, Migrant, and Bilingual Education. Prior to that, she served as the Director of Educational Services for the Educational Improvement Center of Northeast New Jersey, where her responsibilities included the development and implementation of educational improvement agreements with school districts and the development of leadership training programs and materials She has also served as a consultant and facilitator in many school districts, a mathematics chairperson, and a middle school teacher.

Eunice Zita Pruitt is an educational consultant and is Director of Professional Development for Corn Associates, Inc. Her current areas of focus are helping schools to align their curriculum and assessment practices with state core curriculum standards and guiding teachers in self-study as they seek to improve their programs. She also conducts workshops and seminars on leadership for principals, supervisors, and aspiring leaders.

A graduate of Hunter College, she obtained her doctoral degree in educational administration from Teachers College, Columbia University. Dr. Pruitt has been an elementary school teacher in New York and New Jersey. She has also served as Administrative Assistant to the Superintendent and as an elementary school principal for many years in Teaneck, New Jersey, where she used many of the strategies discussed in this book.

Dr. Pruitt has taught graduate courses at the City University of New York in leadership, educational planning, and systems problem solving. She has presented at national, state, and local conferences, and has written several articles. Dr. Pruitt has been honored frequently by community groups for her outstanding work in education.

1

The Professional Learning Community

An Overview

PREVIEW OF THE CHAPTER

Today, a great deal is known about what leads to school improvement and about the change process in schools. In the current literature, there is extensive discussion of the learning community as an effective model for fostering school improvement and general consensus about high-quality learning activities as essential factors in the improvement of teaching and learning. This chapter provides the theoretical basis for an understanding of the learning community as a metaphor for schools and the rationale for the strategies that lead to schools characterized by collaboration, shared leadership, and ongoing learning. The evolution of the learning community in the research literature is explored and an in-depth discussion of the characteristics and impact of the learning community on students, teachers, and staff is provided. The chapter specifically addresses the following questions:

- What is a learning community?
- What are the characteristics of a learning community?
- How is student achievement affected by the learning community model?
- How are teachers affected by the learning community?
- How do reflection and reflective practice contribute to the building of learning communities?

WHAT IS A LEARNING COMMUNITY?

Dr. Karla Brownstone is just beginning her tenure as the superintendent of the Menlo School District, an urban/suburban-type district where achievement scores and teacher morale have been on the decline for several years. The former superintendent had a highly directive leadership style that limited his ability to improve the schools and resulted in a high turnover in the administrative staff. In her initial meetings with the Board of Education, teachers, and other staff and community members, Dr. Brownstone had shared her vision of providing the kind of leadership that would facilitate the transformation of each of the district's schools into learning communities. Her ideas had generated some interest among the district's building principals and supervisors.

When she initially toured the schools in the district, the superintendent observed that the teachers in the elementary and middle schools all taught in self-contained classrooms in which the children were homogeneously grouped. In a survey conducted by the district staff, the teachers had overwhelmingly indicated their approval of the manner in which students were assigned to their classes.

Superintendent Brownstone found that most curriculum and instruction decisions were made by a curriculum planning committee chaired by Jack Carson, the Director of Curriculum and Instruction and composed of central office staff curriculum planning committee. The declining achievement scores in mathematics had recently led the planning committee to implement a new mathematics program in the district. The central office personnel were ready for a change that would lead to an improvement in school climate, more effective teaching, and higher academic achievement in their schools. The achievement data had led them to realize that the strategy they were using had not improved teaching and learning in Menlo's schools. Dr. Brownstone is now planning a series of meetings with the teachers and staff in each school to share with them the meaning of a school as a community of learners. What information should she include in her presentation?

Over the past several decades, the research literature on school improvement and school reform has focused on the characteristics of effective schools and the importance of the principal's leadership role and behavior (Purkey & Smith, 1983; Sergiovanni, 1992). The metaphor for schools which dominated the literature during this period was the notion of schools as

---

Information Online 1.1

Do you want to know more about Senge's ideas on the learning organization? Read M. K. Smith's (2001) article *Peter Senge and the Learning Organization*, at http://www.infed.org/thinkers/senge.htm. Information is provided on the five disciplines (systems thinking, personal mastery, mental models, building shared vision, and team learning) which Senge identifies as the core disciplines in shaping a learning organization.

---

formal organizations. The 1990 publication of Peter Senge's work *The Fifth Discipline* led members of the education community to explore new ways of improving how schools operated and the professionalism of teachers and administrators.

Senge's Learning Organization

Senge (1990), whose focus was on corporations rather than schools, argued that if corporations are to survive, they must change themselves into learning organizations that recognize the threats to their survival and the opportunities for their continued growth. He describes five learning disciplines that must effectively be employed to build a learning organization: (1) personal mastery, (2) mental models, (3) team learning, (4) building shared vision, and (5) systems thinking. In implementing these principles, people learn from each other and develop more effective ways of doing things. Practical ideas and tools that can be used to help educators apply the five learning disciplines in schools can be found in *Schools That Learn* (Senge et al., 2000).

In recent years, the school reform literature has begun to reflect a view of schools as communities of learners. Transforming a school into a learning community, however, can pose some significant challenges for educators. Building a learning organization requires organizational members to have access to such resources as time to collaborate, ongoing leadership support, information, and ready access to colleagues (Senge, 1994). A lack of meaningful opportunities to engage in learning activities can limit the capacity of schools to become learning organizations (Lashway, 1997). In our experience, schools typically do not encourage shared thinking; rather, teachers are generally free to make their own instructional decisions.

The above-stated views on schools as learning communities beg the question, *What does a learning community school look like?* A snapshot of such a school, in which one of the authors served as the college supervisor of administrative interns, is provided below.

A Snapshot of a Learning Community School

Walking about the halls of a New York City high school, I noticed that in many ways this school was different from others. The four-year-old school, which was housed in an older school building, lacked many of the facilities of other newly founded schools in the city. However, I was struck by the fact that the doors to the classrooms were always open and the students and teachers were all deeply involved in learning activities. During my twice-a-month visits to the school, as I freely moved from classroom to classroom, it struck me that an unusual amount of student talk took place in the classrooms. Students felt comfortable in probing for understanding. They freely entered into dialogue with their teachers; students and teachers alike challenged one another's thinking with their questions. The environment was exciting, and I came to the realization that the students in this school were continually searching for meaning and accepting responsibility for their own learning. I rarely saw this level of student engagement in the other high schools I visited. More often, students were treated as receptacles for information, and instruction was more likely to be teacher-centered and narrowly planned around the state testing program.

When this school first opened, the teachers had been permitted to make their own decisions collaboratively about the kind of programs they wanted to implement. The faculty had decided to utilize a thematic interdisciplinary curriculum incorporating a team-teaching approach. Each team of teachers decided on the norms that specified how the teams would work together.

The program had been implemented after a year of training. The teachers had selected key staff from another well-regarded school that used a collaborative approach to providing professional development. During the period of training, as they interacted with teachers from the other school, made interschool visits, and learned more about team teaching and thematic curriculum development and implementation, the faculty had come to realize that they had mutual responsibility for their own learning as well as the learning of all the students on their teams. Over time, this approach to teaching and learning resulted in a level of interdependence among the faculty that fostered collaboration within and among the teaching teams. Additionally, they discovered that reflecting on their ideas and activities and making and carrying out decisions were intellectually stimulating and motivating. The decisions they made affected the breadth and depth of their students' learning as well as how they felt about themselves as educators.

A visit to the teachers' room revealed the same level of interest in learning as I found when visiting classrooms. The conversations of the teachers were invariably concerned with the plans being made for their classes. A bulletin board in the teachers' room announced various activities that were planned around teaching and learning issues. Reminders were posted about regularly scheduled school leadership team meetings, study groups meetings, activities for new teachers, meetings of the peer coaching team, and purely social events. With the support of the principal, all of these activities were collaboratively planned and led by teachers.

One of the building principal's priorities is to provide the instructional support that the teachers felt they needed. At the recommendation of the faculty, positions for half-time coordinators of technology, science, and audiovisual and instructional materials have been carved out of the available teaching positions. The coordinators are available to support teachers in all content areas and to provide for or arrange learning resources as requested by the teaching teams.

The entire faculty keeps its focus on student learning by taking advantage of the available opportunities to talk about and learn about teaching strategies and their students' needs. The principal provides the teachers with available achievement data, which the teams use to plan for instruction. On a regular basis, they collaboratively analyze the data from tests developed by the teams to make plans for instruction. The teachers have become socialized to the extent that they maintain open classrooms, which other teachers can enter and observe on an informal basis.

All activities are built around the school's core mission, which is focused on advancing student achievement. Plans have been made for a small group of teachers to meet to reexamine and update the existing mission statement They will share it with the teachers at a faculty meeting. The faculty will discuss and modify it, if necessary, before moving to adopt the statement. The principal plans to carry this

process out every two years, as she believes the mission as stated helps
some of the faculty stay focused.

Clearly, the school described in the above snapshot has learning as its
focus. How, though, do we define a learning community and what learning community characteristics have become embedded in the culture of
this school?

Defining Learning Community

The term *learning community* has taken on a variety of meanings in the
literature. In *Improving Schools From Within*, Roland Barth (1990) describes
a community of learners as "a place where students and adults alike are
engaged as active learners in matters of special importance to them and
where everyone is thereby encouraging everyone else's learning" (p. 9).
He also explores the role of teachers and principals as learners and the
importance of cooperative and collegial relationships as important aspects
of community.

In *Recreating Schools*, Myers and Simpson (1998) describe learning communities as "cultural settings in which everyone learns, in which every
individual is an integral part, and in which every participant is responsible for both the learning and the overall well-being of everyone else" (p. 2).

Speck (1999), who asserts that shaping a learning community is the
most pressing task of the building principal, describes a learning community as follows:

> A school learning community is one that promotes and values
> learning as an ongoing, active collaborative process with dynamic
> dialogue by teachers, students, staff, principal, parents, and the
> school community to improve the quality of learning and life
> within the school. Developing schools where every aspect of the
> community nourishes learning and helping everyone who comes
> into contact with the school to contribute to that learning commu-
> nity are important concepts. (p. 8)

As defined above by Speck, members of a learning community are
mutually responsible for building the community.

Thus, building a school learning community becomes the collective
pursuit of the principal, teachers, students, parents, and all other community members. To accomplish their goal, this group must carry on conversations about the fundamental issues that influence the quality of the
available learning opportunities offered to all members of the school

Information Online 1.2

Read the ERIC Digest *Creating a Learning Organization*, at http//eric.uorgeon.edu/publications/digests/digest 121.htm.

   Based on the content of the digest, discuss the following questions:

- What factors pose as constraints to the building of a learning community in your school?
- What factors present opportunities for building a learning community in your school?

---

community. Importantly, Collay and her associates (Collay, Dunlap, Enloe, & Gagnon, 1998) note that not only are individual and collective growth cherished in a learning community, but the processes for attaining that growth are also valued.

WHAT ARE THE CHARACTERISTICS OF A LEARNING COMMUNITY?

The literature identifies characteristics that are associated with the development and maintenance of communities of learners. Our discussion in this section is based on the work of Kruse et al. (1995) in *Professionalism and Community: Perspectives on Reforming Urban Schools*. The characteristics that they identify (Figure 1.1) serve as the theoretical basis for the ideas and activities described throughout this book.

Kruse, Louis, and Bryk: Characteristics of a Professional Community

   A professional community, as identified by Kruse et al. (1995), has as its focus the cultivation of learning and interaction among teachers and administrators so as to improve teaching and learning outcomes for students and for the school community at large. As a result of extensive research, they cite five elements of a professional community: (1) reflective dialogue, (2) focus on student learning, (3) interaction among teacher

Figure 1.1 Kruse, Louis, and Bryk (1995) Formulation of the Professional Community

	Dimensions of the Professional Community
Characteristics	Reflective dialogue
	Collective focus on student learning
	Deprivatization of practice
	Collaboration
	Shared values and norms
Structural Conditions	Time to meet and discuss
	Physical proximity
	Interdependent teaching roles
	Teacher empowerment/school autonomy
	Communication structures
Human/Social Resources	Openness to improvement
	Trust and respect
	Supportive leadership
	Socialization
	Cognitive/skill base

SOURCE: "An Emerging Framework for Analyzing School-Based Professional Community," Kruse, Louis, & Bryk (1995). Copyright © by Corwin Press. Reprinted/Adapted by permission of Corwin Press.

colleagues, (4) collaboration, and (5) shared values and norms. Each element is briefly defined below.

Reflective dialogue is described as those conversations which focus on teaching behaviors and learning outcomes in order to encourage teachers to discuss their teaching practices and collaborate on how they can be improved.

In explaining the element of a *focus on student learning,* Kruse et al. (1995) emphasize that the purpose of all actions in a professional community should be the growth and development of all the students. This element is characterized by ongoing conversations and decision making about curriculum, teaching, and learning that concentrate on student outcomes.

It is through *interactions among teachers* that professional relationships are developed that encourage teachers to share ideas, learn from one another, and help out their colleagues. This element, which is also described as the *deprivatization of practice,* includes behaviors that lead teachers to open their classrooms for observation by other teachers.

Traditionally, teachers work alone in their classrooms, where they create a learning environment for up to 30 or more students at a time. Kruse et al. (1995) indicate that *collaboration* occurs when teachers share instructional strategies and techniques, make decisions about instructional issues, and come up with ideas that enhance learning for all members of the school community.

The characteristic *shared values and norms* expresses the idea that the members of the professional community have reached agreement about the mission of their school and the values and norms that are to shape their behaviors as professionals.

Louis and Kruse (1995) also cite five structural conditions and five human/social resources that are essential for establishing professional community. The structural conditions include (1) providing adequate time for teachers to meet and exchange ideas; (2) locating teachers physically closely to one another so that they can observe and interact with peers; (3) ensuring teacher empowerment and school autonomy so that teachers may feel free to do what they believe to be best for their students; (4) creating schoolwide communication structures, including regularly established meetings that are devoted to teaching, learning, and other professional issues; and (5) employing methods, such as team teaching, that require teachers to practice their craft together.

The human/social resources consist of (1) support for teachers who are open to improvement, as demonstrated by a readiness to analyze, reflect on, and try out new approaches to teaching; (2) trust in and respect for the abilities of all members of the learning community; and (3) support from those in leadership positions; (4) processes for socializing teachers into the collegial school culture; and (5) opportunities to acquire new knowledge and skills needed to build a learning community.

As schools work toward developing learning communities, it is important to keep in mind that shared values and norms are the cornerstone on which the community rests and from which the other dimensions will take root (Kruse et al., 1995). At the same time, teachers can only feel empowered to act on their shared beliefs if the school and district leadership offer them the autonomy, the opportunity, and the time to meet that they need to make decisions about improving teaching and learning.[1]

Standards, Accountability, and the Learning Community

Many schools and school districts have welcomed the standards movement as a vehicle for educational reform. Unquestionably, standards-based accountability, together with the high-stakes testing movement, is having a deeply felt impact on the way in which schools operate. The question that each school must address, however, is this: *How can we make certain that our students are offered the instructional programs needed to meet the rigorous standards established by their school districts?*

Information Online 1.3

Visit the Website *Development of Materials to Support the Formation of Learning Communities* at http://www. nwrel.org/scpd/scc/natspec/formlc.shtml. This site contains a set of detailed materials designed to promote informed conversation in staff development sessions on developing learning communities. The characteristics that guide the materials are Hord's Attributes of Learning Communities, but the materials can be readily adopted to other learning community models. The staff development resources include:

- A description of the Story Investigation Approach, which allows participants to learn from one another by telling stories that reflect their experiences in a school with learning community characteristics.
- Staff development activities that promote dialogue about learning communities. These activities are designed to prepare participants to successfully engage in dialogue.
- Sample overheads that can be used or adapted for professional development activities.

The learning community model provides some answers to this question. When teachers in a learning community collaborate and resolve issues around what content to teach and how best to teach it, they are searching for a common understanding of what effective teaching looks like for all children in their school community. The collegial decisions they make are more likely than traditional approaches to offer every child the opportunity to learn because their collective focus is always on the outcomes of instruction (Little, 1990). Accountability for standards becomes a community issue as teams of teachers work together to accomplish their shared vision.

Clearly, schools with learning community characteristics offer a school climate in which students can perform to standards. They offer a high-quality learning environment for teachers, which translates into greater learning opportunities for students.

Information Online 1.4

Visit the Website *Transforming Learning Communities* at http://www.ode.state.oh.us/tlc. This site describes a research project on school change and school improvement at a cohort of schools in Ohio. The study addresses the question, "How do learning communities develop and what can be done to strengthen and speed up their urgent reforms?" Read the findings of the study.

- Are any of the important issues discussed in the study found in your school?
- Which characteristics of learning communities are found in these schools and to what extent?
- Identify some steps taken to bring about change in the schools.
- Describe the impact of the change on the teachers and students.

HOW IS STUDENT ACHIEVEMENT AFFECTED BY THE LEARNING COMMUNITY MODEL?

The ultimate purpose of the movement to the learning community model is to improve learning opportunities and outcomes for students. Teachers in learning community schools engage in collaborative activities that are directed toward helping them to improve their instructional practices. Their students are likely to be the beneficiaries as the teachers share ideas, learn innovative and better ways of teaching, and try the newly learned approaches in the classroom.

A recent study, which explored the link between teacher learning, teacher instructional behavior, and student outcomes, showed that engaging in an ongoing learning process led teachers to identify and carry out practices that resulted in increased graduation rates, improved college admission rates, and higher academic achievement for their students (Ancess, 2000).

The Evergreen Elementary School in Plainfield, New Jersey provides evidence of how the shift to a learning community model can affect the academic achievement of students. For the past four years, the district has focused its resources on improving literacy instruction. Evergreen, under the leadership of its principal, Gloria Williams, has as its goal that all its students score at the *proficient* or *advanced proficient* level on the state Elementary School Proficiency Assessment.

Many of the learning community characteristics have become part of Evergreen's culture. Time has been structured for teachers to meet regularly in grade-level teams to address teaching and learning issues and to prepare lessons that address student needs. These collaborative planning meetings are characterized by the use of student data to make instructional decisions.

Study groups have been used in a variety of ways to build community at Evergreen. Teachers have been given journal articles to read and share at grade-level meetings or during the first few minutes of a staff meeting. A separate evening study group was formed, composed of teachers and administrators, who selected the book *Improving Comprehension With Think-Aloud Strategies*, by Jeffrey D. Wilhelm (2001). Evergreen parents are also engaged in a book club, which meets on a monthly basis. These strategies have provided teachers and parents with time to develop the common understanding and language needed to collaborate and discuss the improvement of student reading. The study groups are part of the principal's efforts to provide ongoing learning opportunities for all members of the school community.

Study groups are only one vehicle used by Gloria Williams to promote learning and foster collaboration. At Evergreen, ongoing professional development is provided for the staff. Several days of targeted professional development, regularly scheduled grade-level meetings, and weekly staff meetings provide opportunities for teachers to meet, exchange ideas, reflect, and improve instruction. Training in the analysis of data, which is the district's basic strategy for guiding instruction is ongoing. Classrooms that provide good examples of standards-based instruction in literacy are regularly made available for visitation by the staff.

Specifically, how has student achievement at Evergreen been affected by these activities? Over the past four years, Evergreen has experienced steady gains in the percentage of students passing the literacy component of the state assessment program. In the last four years, the percentage of students at Evergreen who have reached the proficient level in literacy has risen from 33.8% to 78% (see Figure 1.2).

Teachers and students regularly hold formal and informal conferences to discuss student progress and how it can be improved. As one strategy, the teachers and students together select work samples for student portfolios. This encourages students to become more involved and to assume an active role in their own learning. These interactions with students can also provide a learning opportunity for Evergreen's teachers, as it provides a form of feedback about their teaching practices.

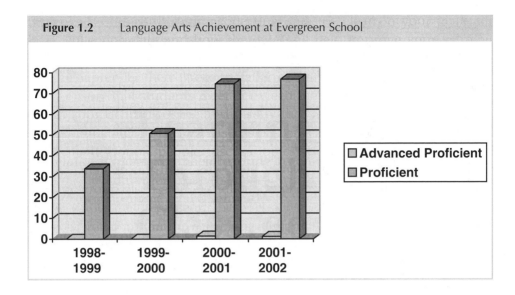

Figure 1.2 Language Arts Achievement at Evergreen School

At least one hour each day during the literacy instructional block and once a week with the school leadership team the principal conducts focus walks around the school. This daily and intensive attention to literacy instruction on the part of the school's leader reinforces staff commitment to issues of teaching and learning.

Visit the Website of the Plainfield New Jersey public schools at http://www.plainfilednjk12.org/ for additional information and data on how the district focus on literacy and the learning community characteristics have led to a steady improvement in literacy scores on the state Elementary School Proficiency Assessment.

HOW ARE TEACHERS AFFECTED BY THE LEARNING COMMUNITY?

The transformation of a school into a professional learning community has profound effects on the members of a school community. Based on the characteristics identified by Kruse et al. (1995) and Hord (1997), the community of learners movement recasts the roles, rules, and relationships that exist between and among teachers, administrators, students, and other community members.

The emerging picture of schools as learning communities reveals that the attributes of learning community schools have a significant influence on the daily work lives of teachers. The influence on teachers can be grouped into five categories: (1) teachers as colleagues, (2) teachers as leaders,

(3) teachers as learners, (4) teachers as pedagogues, and (5) teacher-parent relationships.

Teachers as Colleagues

Our experiences as facilitators of school change projects bear out that the dialogue that occurs when isolation is reduced is perceived by teachers as an exchange of valuable information with peers. Teachers have often informed us that consistently talking about their teaching permits them to learn new things, to contribute to each others' learning and development, and to improve the quality of their working relationships. This sustained collegiality leads teachers to become more aware of their obligation to work together to resolve schoolwide concerns as well as issues associated with their own teaching behaviors (Barth, 1990; DuFour & Eaker, 1998).

Teachers as Leaders

When teachers fulfill their commitment, individually or as a group, to take responsibility for the well-being of their schools, they are exercising their leadership roles (Barth, 1990). They are more likely to understand and be committed to making meaningful and long-lasting change and to work toward accomplishing the mission and goals of their schools (Hord, 1997). Their capacity to fulfill leadership roles is enhanced by their understanding of what it is that they want to accomplish (DuFour & Eaker, 1998).

Teachers as Learners

Teachers in learning community schools are found to focus on learning as opposed to teaching. Their learning serves to inform their teaching and to generate new knowledge and views about teaching and learning and the part they play in helping all their students to be successful learners (DuFour & Eaker, 1998; Hord, 1997).

Teachers as Pedagogues

When teachers collaborate as part of a schoolwide community, they spend time sharing teaching strategies, planning for instruction, and looking for new ways to improve learning (Kruse et al. 1995). They work with administrators to identify what students should know and be able to do. In our work, we find that they take on greater responsibility for student outcomes and for school improvement. As one teacher wrote after a year-long series of professional development sessions,

Because we meet a lot to talk and plan together for our teaching, I have a better grasp on how to teach the content we are supposed to teach. We know that our students are learning more. In the long run, we expect to see better achievement scores on the state tests. For the first time, I feel comfortable helping some of the less experienced teachers with how to teach the content. Actually, I enjoy teaching more than in the past. I believe that I have the help I need to help my students reach the standards set by the district. Most of the teachers feel more positive about student outcomes. Actually, the more I learn about teaching, the more I like teaching because the more my students learn.

Teacher-Parent Relationships

Students, parents, and teachers benefit when parents assume the role of learners. Their involvement expands learning opportunities for students, because they become more knowledgeable about teaching and learning (Speck, 1999). When parents understand the work of the learning community, they can become advocates for the instructional changes that teachers put into place for their children.

As the group's conversations became more spontaneous, they felt freer to publicly discuss their beliefs about standards and their instructional needs. Individual members of the group began to bring ideas and questions about teaching to the group. They began to share ideas about what worked and what did not work in their classrooms. Prodded by the facilitator, they gradually generated a set of questions to guide their reflections.

When members tried out an activity suggested by the group, follow-up reflective questions were raised, such as, *Do you think the activity helped to improve student learning? Were there any unexpected outcomes? What changes could be made in the activity to make the teaching process better?* Over time, as they learned more about teaching and learning, group members became more committed to the reflective process.

HOW DO REFLECTION AND REFLECTIVE PRACTICE CONTRIBUTE TO THE BUILDING OF LEARNING COMMUNITIES?

The process of reflection provides teachers with the opportunity to cast light on and make sense of what they have learned while engaging in collaborative dialogue with their peers. The importance of reflection has been affirmed by the Interstate New Teacher Assessment and Support Consortium (INTASC), a program of the Council of Chief State School Officers, which has developed 10 standards for licensing new teachers. INTASC Standard #9 states,

> The teacher is a reflective practitioner who continually evaluates the effects of his/her choices and actions on others (students, parents, and other professionals in the learning community) and who actively seeks out opportunities to grow professionally. (p. 31)

The reflective process is critical for three reasons: first, the outcome is improved student learning; second, as a result of reflection, teachers can acquire the working knowledge they need to improve their teaching practice; and, third, reflection contributes to the building of community (York-Barr, Sommers, Ghere, & Montie, 2001). As pointed out in *Schools That Learn*, what most experienced teachers know about teaching and learning is acquired through systematic, ongoing reflection on classroom and schoolwide practices (Senge et al., 2000). Their extensive knowledge base and deeper understanding of teaching and learning are acquired by closely examining and questioning their teaching behaviors.

Group reflection and self-reflection are elements of many of the collaborative activities discussed throughout this book. Team meetings, committee meetings, study groups, pre-/postobservation conferences, grade-level meetings, portfolio development, walk-throughs, and a host of other community-building strategies involve teachers in the process of reflecting on their professional practice. We have observed that, when group reflection occurs in structured activities, teachers are empowered by the support and feedback received from their peers. As a result, they are more likely to try new ways of teaching. Exactly what does group reflection look like in a learning community?

One of the authors served as the facilitator for a group of high school mathematics teachers who wanted to engage in discussions about their instructional practices. The group had been meeting every other week for about two months to discuss activities that would help them to teach to the mathematics content standards. When they began the process, the teachers were hesitant about making contributions to the conversation. Once the group was trained in group processes, they began to develop trust and to feel more comfortable with one another.

As the group's conversations became more spontaneous, they felt freer to publicly discuss their beliefs about standards and their instructional needs. Individual members of the group began to bring ideas and questions about teaching to the group. They began to talk about what worked

---

Tips for Leaders 1.1

To encourage reflection among your teachers,

- Look for opportunities to openly discuss classroom issues of importance to teachers, such as test scores, student motivation, and so forth.
- Invite a guest facilitator to dialogue with teachers on an issue of importance to them.
- Where appropriate, participate with teachers and others in your school in a reflective practice group.

---

and what did not work in their classrooms. Prodded by the facilitator, they focused on teaching and learning rather than on the students' backgrounds, their parents, and socioeconomic factors as issues related to student achievement.

They gradually generated a set of questions to guide their reflections. When members tried out an activity suggested by the group, follow-up reflective questions were raised, such as, Do you think the activity helped to improve student learning? Were there any unexpected outcomes? What changes could be made in the activity to make the teaching process better? Over time, as they learned more about teaching and learning, group members became more committed to the reflective process.

Reflective Cycle Process

Group reflection involves members of a learning group subjecting their personal views and practices about teaching and learning to critical analysis, and it should result in the application of what they have learned to improve outcomes for students (York-Barr et al., 2001).

Many models of reflective practice are described in the literature. The six-stage process of reflective practice described below can be adapted for groups or individuals. In addition to being influenced by our own experiences and the work of Carol Rodgers (2002), the process has been adapted from the work of York-Barr et al. (2001). The six steps are as follows.

1. *Identifying a Practice/Product for Group Reflection.* A team may select or a teacher may share a teaching practice or product to be examined collaboratively. An instructional program, student work, a

classroom teaching practices, or a specific lesson plan are all examples of what may be selected for the reflective process.

2. *Describing the Practice/Product Selected for Group Reflection.* The activity, practice, or product selected for review must be carefully described so that all members of the team share a common understanding of the item being reviewed. Members of the team can pose questions to obtain an objective picture of teachers' thoughts and feelings about the practice or product and how it affects student outcomes in the learning community. It is important that sufficient time be allowed for this step to uncover information that can be used for meaningful reflection.

3. *Examining the Practice/Product Selected for Reflection.* During the third stage, the team engages in a reflective dialogue that sets the stage for collaborative learning. Members of the group must openly but courteously share their thoughts and feelings about the product, about what has occurred, and about what could have been done differently. Questions around why the particular instructional practice or product was chosen may be posed. *How did students respond to its use? What did the teacher learn from its use? Does it help students to achieve a particular district standard?* The team may identify what worked, what did not work, and what needs to be changed or modified. Based on the discussion, new ways of carrying out the process or using the product are identified. Finally, they should summarize what has been learned during this stage.

4. *Acting on What Is Learned During Reflection.* Based on what is learned through reflection, a set of actions to improve the teaching practice or product is developed and carried out by the teacher.

5. *Assessing the Outcome of the Action Plan.* Collective learning is the focus of the fifth step. After the recommendations have been tried, the outcome of the planned actions should be discussed. The team should reflect on how the planned changes affected student and teacher learning. Individual members of the team should describe what they learned from the process.

6. *Building Community Through the Cycle of Reflection.* Community building will be promoted by preparing and disseminating a list of what has been learned through collaborative reflection. Other members of the team should be encouraged to share instructional practices or products and to repeat steps 1 through 5 to promote the ongoing building of professional community.

A learning community is nurtured by ongoing, structured activities that require teachers to engage in cycles of reflection through which they can learn from one another's practice. As Kruse et al. (1995) point out, "In organized settings reflection becomes a joint responsibility as teachers work toward a better understanding of their own learning and abilities" (p. 30).

For extensive, in-depth information on reflection and reflective practice, we recommend *Reflective Practice to Improve Schools: An Action Guide for Educators* (York-Barr et al., 2001). A review of this work will provide ideas that can be used to prepare some questions to guide the discussion at each of the above steps in the process.

Some Final Thoughts on Reflection

Trust building is an important aspect of the reflective group process that must be addressed. When teachers sit down to reflect on one another's teaching practices or activities, the members of the group may feel threatened. It is not characteristic of teachers who traditionally carry out their professional roles in isolation to publicly discuss concerns they may have about their teaching. As in the example above, leaders should take into consideration the fact that levels of trust have a significant impact on a team's ability to engage in reflective practice and that, in fact, the inability to trust may delay progress toward community building. Useful strategies for building trust are discussed in Chapter 2.

It is also important to keep in mind that controversy, another aspect of the group reflective process, can be useful because it develops deeper understandings. Different perspectives enrich conversations and help a team look at teaching and learning more deeply.

A Teacher Reflects

In our work with schools, we have found that teachers' sense of professionalism is enhanced when they work as colleagues, make instructional decisions, and develop a sense of community. One of the teachers in a school in which we serve as facilitators shared the following eloquent statement with us from her professional journal:

Our school has developed clear shared mission and vision statements. Our work was accomplished with the help of an outside facilitator and a newly appointed, understanding, committed and very, very patient principal. During the principal's first year, the teachers were given a lot of opportunities to work together on projects in which they were interested. Slowly, as they began to feel more comfortable and valued, more teachers and parents became interested in the direction the school was taking.

I think it took about three years before I could see the beginning of definite changes in the way things were being done in our school, changes in the way things were being done by the teachers. It was worth the time that we put into the process. Now many teachers are willing to work together to solve the problems that come up in the school, to improve their teaching, and to try new ways of doing things. We really enjoy talking and reading about teaching and learning and visiting each others' classrooms. Our principal is very good about scheduling time so that we can meet to talk about our ideas and participate in staff development activities.

All of the staff development in our school is planned by a committee of teachers and a lot of it is done by the teachers themselves. We follow up on the training sessions in our peer group meetings and for the first time teachers really take the training seriously. I think that our students and parents are happier campers now because they have a more professional staff. We have made a good beginning. We still have a lot of challenges, but we are satisfied with our work and enjoy coming to school. It's all about learning new things.

CONCLUSION

Building learning communities requires a shift from the paradigm of schools as bureaucracies to a vision of schools as communities. Teachers in learning community schools work in teams where, collaboratively, through sustained reflection and inquiry, they learn by sharing professional practices. As educators collaboratively engage in conversation and deliberate about teaching and learning, they gain new knowledge and discover original ways to resolve instructional issues. In the process, they develop a shared vision and strengthen their ability to achieve the vision that they want for their schools.

They are supported in their learning efforts by leaders who provide the encouragement, the time, and other conditions that permit them to collaborate, visit one another's classrooms, and experiment with new teaching strategies. The culture of a community of learners permits the teachers in a school to view themselves as members of a team of learners and leaders, rather than as participants in the traditional leader-follower roles.

ACTIVITIES

Assessment of Implementation
Learning Community Characteristics

Use the instrument below to evaluate the extent to which the characteristics of learning communities are found in your school. The instrument is not all-inclusive: Its purpose is to stimulate your thinking and provide a focus for a discussion of your school's implementation of the characteristics. The instrument should be completed anonymously. The teachers may want to prepare an item analysis ranking the descriptors for each learning community attribute based on the percentage of faculty agreement. In reflecting on the data, it is important to discuss the meaning of the characteristics as well as the meaning of the items. The items are based on the professional community attributes identified Kruse et al. (1995) and Hord (1997).

Each item is rated on a scale of 1 to 3 (1 = *disagree*, 2 = *somewhat agree*, 3 = *agree*).

Shared Leadership in This School

1. The principal and supervisors encourage and support the development of teacher leaders.   1   2   3
2. Teachers are encouraged and provided time to coach and mentor other teachers.   1   2   3
3. Teachers can serve as heads of committees and as decision makers.   1   2   3
4. The recommendations made by teachers are given serious consideration and support.   1   2   3
5. Opportunities are provided for training in shared decision making and collaborative planning.   1   2   3

Collaboration in This School

1. Faculty, staff, and community members carry on conversations about teaching and learning.   1   2   3
2. Faculty, staff, and community members work together to solve identified problems.   1   2   3
3. Teachers dialogue across grade levels and content areas to promote understanding and share ideas.   1   2   3
4. In their classrooms, teachers try out the ideas which they share in their conversations.   1   2   3
5. The teachers had input in selecting the decision-making process used in the school.   1   2   3

Shared Values/Vision in This School

1. Faculty/staff members have participated in developing the school's vision statement.   1   2   3
2. Student learning is the consistent focus of the teachers and other staff members.   1   2   3

3. Channels for formal and informal communication among faculty/staff members have been established.	1	2	3
4. Parents and other community members have been involved in developing the vision statement.	1	2	3
5. The teachers had input in selecting the decision-making process used in the school.	1	2	3

Structural/Social Supports in This School

1. Adequate time is provided for teachers/staff to meet and discuss issues.	1	2	3
2. Schedules have been established which reduce teacher isolation.	1	2	3
3. Teachers have some input in selecting new teachers, administrators, and other staff members.	1	2	3
4. Time is available for the faculty to meet and discuss issues.	1	2	3
5. Trust and respect are demonstrated among the teachers and administrators.	1	2	3

Shared Practice in This School

1. Faculty and staff members help one another to reflect upon and improve their practice.	1	2	3
2. Teachers have the opportunity to identify the focus of professional development activities.	1	2	3
3. In-service training is proved for parents on a regularly scheduled basis.	1	2	3
4. Supervisors and administrators participate in professional development activities with the teachers.	1	2	3
5. Regularly scheduled grade-level and content-level meetings are conducted by teachers.	1	2	3

Change in the Menlo School District

As the new Superintendent of the Menlo School District, you are going to conduct a meeting with the district's elementary school teachers. The topic of the meeting is *What Is a Learning Community?* Use the information provided in the chapter and the Online Information to prepare the outline of a 30-minute presentation that you will make to the teachers.

NOTE

1. The material on characteristics of a professional community has been adapted from "An Emerging Framework for Analyzing School-Based Professional Community," by Kruse et al. (1995, pp. 26–40). Copyright © by Corwin Press. Adapted by permission of Corwin Press.

2

Learning Through Shared Leadership

PREVIEW OF THE CHAPTER

A legion of writers and researchers have identified leadership as an essential ingredient in the school improvement process (Hallinger & Heck, 1996). The leadership role of the principal is a pivotal aspect of efforts to build a learning community. However, attempts at building community and addressing the learning needs of students and teachers are frequently hampered by a lack of knowledge of the behaviors that constitute effective leadership and by competing visions of what effective schools and classrooms should look like.

While the traditional bureaucratic practice in schools has been for those in leadership positions to make decisions and to manage teacher behavior, a shift in the view of leadership is occurring that stresses "developing a vision that involves followers, inspires them, and motivates their efforts. It is the shared vision of a better school that has the power to transform the relationships between the teachers and the principal, for example, uniting them in mutually sharing the work required to achieve the vision" (Owens, 2001, p. 251). Much of the school improvement literature today reflects this perspective.

As the view of schools shifts from that of schools as organizations to schools as learning communities, the model of leadership must shift from centralized decision making to shared leadership. This chapter will address the issue of leadership in a learning community by addressing the following questions:

- What are the roles of educational leaders in a learning community?
- What steps must a principal take to develop a shared mission and vision?
- What strategies can educational leaders use to communicate and sustain the vision?
- How do principals build the trust that contributes to improved student achievement?
- What communication skills do leaders need to successfully lead learning communities?
- What do leaders need to know about the change process?
- How do you begin the process of building a learning community?

WHAT ARE THE ROLES OF EDUCATIONAL LEADERS IN A LEARNING COMMUNITY?

Joseph Rios has been the principal at School #5 in the Menlo School District for five years. Although he is excited about some of the ideas the new superintendent, Dr. Karla Brownstone, is bringing to the district, he does not fully understand why she places so much emphasis on changing the way leadership is provided in the schools. Whereas she discussed the importance of leadership at every meeting that she held with the principals, Principal Rios rarely gave much thought to the topic. He has always used a written survey to get his teachers' recommendations before he makes important decisions about teaching, professional development, and the organizational issues that affect his school. He also believes that the school has improved somewhat since he became principal. He is aware that there are some significant problems yet to be solved at School #5, but he attributes them to the absence of a sense of commitment on the part of a group of uninvolved teachers.

Although the school has a reputation for being well managed, the achievement scores still lag considerably below the district-mandated standards. Two years ago, with the help of the district reading coordinator, the principal had selected and implemented a new literature-based reading program which addressed the literacy standards adopted by the district. Although the teachers did not greet the arrival of the program with any observable enthusiasm, they are implementing it in their classrooms. Rios considers this to be an accomplishment and has a great deal of pride in the program that he selected.

At Rios's evaluation meeting with the superintendent, they reviewed the school's achievement scores, discussed the strategies used to improve achievement, and talked about his leadership role in the implementation of the new literacy curriculum. Dr. Brownstone specifically wanted to know about the strategies used to provide opportunities for the teachers to learn more about providing literacy instruction. Principal Rios self-assuredly explained how he regularly reviewed the teachers' lesson plans, consistently monitored classroom instruction, provided feedback, and offered several workshops each year on improving instructional practices. The superintendent advised that he needed to work on his teachers' commitment to the program and get them more involved in discussions about teaching and learning issues. She suggested that he arrange to visit two schools in the district, talk with their principals about how they worked with their teachers, and identify some strategies for getting his teachers more involved. At their next scheduled meeting, he and the superintendent are to discuss what he learned during his school visits and what strategies he plans to use in the new school year.

The pressures experienced by Joseph Rios are similar to the issues confronting building principals around the country. Those in leadership positions are operating in rapidly changing, standards-driven accountability systems that focus on the measurement of the performance of all students. Meeting the educational needs of the diverse cultural groups who populate our schools and ensuring that they all have access to appropriate opportunities to learn calls for those in leadership positions to harness the commitment of and ensure collaboration among all those responsible for providing learning opportunities at each school site.

Defining Leadership in a Learning Community

Educational writers have examined and debated the meaning of leadership and the role of school leaders in the school improvement process from a variety of viewpoints. School leadership models have changed so rapidly over the past few decades that those in leadership positions have been unable to translate one model into practice before a new model emerged in the literature. Our purpose is to clarify the meaning of leadership and to explore leadership strategies related to developing and maintaining a community of learners. Several models exist that can inform and guide the behavior of leaders in a learning community.

Facilitative Leadership

Facilitative leadership is the phrase used by Conley and Goldman (1994) to portray "how principals come to lead without dominating"

(p. 237). They define it as "the behaviors that enhance the collective ability of a school to adapt, solve problems, and improve performance" (p. 238).

Facilitative leadership is evidenced by the principal's behaviors in promoting the development of a shared vision and fostering the growth of teacher-leaders and new leadership structures in their schools. Effective facilitative leaders provide opportunities for staff members to share information and for communication and networking between the school and members of the broader educational community. These principals work at preparing teachers for change through such activities as discussing ideas one-on-one with faculty members, interschool visits, and other professional activities. As they practice collaboration and shared decision making, they facilitate school reform by finding ways of dealing with the restraints imposed by scarce resources and the pressures that arise in a school undergoing change (Conley & Goldman, 1994).[1]

Constructivist Leadership

Linda Lambert's (Lambert et al., 1995) formulation of constructivist leadership associates leadership with the practice of building community and defines it as "the reciprocal processes that enable participants in an educational community to construct meanings that lead toward a common purpose about schooling" (p. 29).

In *Building Leadership Capacity in Schools*, the leadership function is described as "embedded in the school as a whole" (Lambert, 1998, p. 5). It is found in the relationships that are formed among individuals in the school. As the entire school community collaboratively engages in the learning processes—reflection, inquiry, dialogue, and action—in their day-to-day work, they are engaging in the business of leadership, which is the business of learning together for a shared purpose. In describing constructivist leadership, Lambert (1998) further elaborates: "The key notion in this definition is that leadership is about learning together, and constructing meaning and knowledge collectively and collaboratively" (p. 5).

The job of the principal takes on even greater significance in the constructivist leadership model, because developing teachers' leadership capacity poses more of a challenge than simply informing them of what they are required to do. Principals must create and support measures that build the capacity for shared leadership by ensuring that opportunities are provided for collaborative learning and ongoing conversation among members of the school community (Lambert, 1998).[2]

Barth's (1990) work appears to support the constructivist view of leadership. He notes that all teachers can lead and that the principal, in assuming the role of leader, must also take on the role of "head learner" in the learning community.

Tips for Leaders 2.1
Reflecting on Leadership

To reflect on the leadership practices in your school community, visit the Website *Becoming a Community of Learners: Emerging Leadership Practices,* at http://www.ncrel.org/cscd/pubs/lead21/2-1l.htm. A checklist is provided that can be used to prompt the members of your school community to think about how they want leadership functions to be carried out at your school site. Adapt the checklist to address the pressing leadership issues in your school.

Advice to Joseph Rios

Let us go back to School #5 in the Menlo School District to see how the principal, Joseph Rios, might use shared leadership and collaborative learning to turn his teachers' attention to the improvement of the school's literacy program. Among the strategies he could employ are the following:

- Visit several effective schools in the district to discuss leadership strategies with the principals and to obtain first hand knowledge of how they lead their schools.
- Meet individually with every teacher in his school to inquire and learn what they believe about literacy instruction. (A detailed description of a process for conducting conferences with teachers is provided in Chapter 6.)
- Establish a schedule that permits the teachers at each grade level to come together every two weeks to discuss and reflect on teaching and learning issues with a focus on the literacy program. The teachers should be able to select their group leaders, identify the annual objectives for their meetings, and develop their own agendas. They should submit a brief summary of their discussions and recommendations, if any, to the principal at least once a month.

The teachers can now:

- Collaboratively examine their instructional practices, identify teaching and learning problems associated with the new literacy program, and make and carry out some suggestions for program improvement. The decisions that they make will be an outgrowth of the knowledge and skills about teaching and learning that already exist in the group.

- Make plans for and try out new strategies to improve instruction.
- Openly discuss the results with one another and exchange ideas about effective teaching strategies.

Slowly, with the support and encouragement of the principal, their role as leaders in planning for improved teaching and learning will grow.

Using this method, Joseph Rios will create a structure that integrates Lambert's (1998) learning processes—reflection, inquiry, dialogue, and action—into the everyday work life of his teachers. Both he and his teachers can use these processes to fulfill their roles as learners and leaders, and to help all members of the staff to develop leadership skills.

Identifying the Roles of the Principal in a Learning Community School

Many of the leadership constructs in Lambert's work are supported by other writers. In discussing leadership, Speck (1999) points out that, although the process of building a learning community begins with the principal, attending to the needs of all learners cannot be realized through the leadership actions of the building principal alone. This is consistent with Lambert's (1998) notion that leadership needs to be concentrated in the entire school community and that it must come from a group of leaders who are learning and leading together, and who are involved in bringing about change in a school. Based on the work of Speck (1999) and Lambert (1998) and on characteristics of a learning community (see Figure 1.1), we identify the key roles of the principal of a learning community to include the tasks summarized in Figure 2.1. The tasks are discussed in the sections that follow.

WHAT STEPS MUST A PRINCIPAL TAKE TO DEVELOP A SHARED MISSION AND VISION?

In order to begin answering this question, let us visit the Hugo Newman College Preparatory School in New York City.

The school had undergone many changes in leadership over the past 10 years. Teacher morale was extremely low, the achievement scores at the school were well below mandated academic standards, and the school was a potential candidate for takeover by the state. The arrival of a new principal, Dr. Peter McFarlane, set in motion a dramatic improvement in the tone of the school, the morale, and enthusiasm of the teachers, the involvement of parents, and the academic achievement

Figure 2.1	Roles of the Principal in Building a Learning Community

- Building a shared vision, mission, and values
- Communicating the vision
- Developing trust
- Practicing communication skills that foster collaboration and commitment
- Planning and facilitating the change process
- Promoting and development of teachers as collaborative leaders and learners
- Ensuring sustained academic improvement

SOURCE: Some of the ideas in this figure have been adapted from *The Principalship: Building a Learning Community,* Speck (1999). Copyright © 1999. Reprinted by permission of Pearson Education, Inc.

of the students. Interviews conducted with teachers at the school revealed that the primary cause for the responsiveness of the teachers to the new principal was his leadership style. As one teacher commented,

> *Mr. McFarlane is very clear about where he wants to take the school. Everyone likes his approach and the school has changed a lot. The most important thing about him is that he has a sense of direction and he is very supportive of the teachers. The teachers appreciate this. They know that they are an important part of where the school is going. He listens to our ideas and is willing to discuss them with us. Classroom teachers are involved in everything that takes place in the school. For the first time, we feel as if the school is going some place.*

Conversations with several other members of the teaching staff repeatedly surfaced comments about Principal McFarlane's leadership. According to one teacher, "Dr. McFarlane talks about learning and teaching in a way that is meaningful for what we needed to accomplish in the classroom." The teachers are offered many learning opportunities through the professional development program provided by an energetic staff developer. McFarlane uses committees of teachers who meet twice a month to collaboratively make decisions about everything from technology to parental involvement. It is through the work accomplished by the committee structure that the energy of the teachers is mobilized, that they take on a leadership role in the school, that the vision is refined, and that a shared vision emerges. The attribute, however, that usually surfaced first in the conversations with Principal McFarlane's staff was his vision, which the staff has come to share.

A shared vision is an important element of a dynamic learning community. How does a leader go about the process of developing mission and vision statements?

Defining a Mission Statement

A mission statement is a brief, succinct statement that explains the purpose for which a school exists. In a learning community, the mission statement describes the school's collective purpose. Developing a compelling mission statement in which all stakeholders can share and which can guide the school over the long term can be realized in several ways. Some schools involve the entire community in crafting such a statement; others assign the work to a task force.

At the Hugo Newman College Preparatory School, where the achievement scores are improving each year, the mission is stated in the form of the theme *Where Excellence in Education Is Our Choice.* The principal uses this theme often in meetings with parents and other visitors. Interviews with teachers in the school reveal that they carry out this mission by sharing ideas and engaging in collaborative planning to ensure that all students have opportunities to learn.

Defining Shared Vision

Simply stated, a shared vision is a shared image of what you desire your school to look like in the future (Wallace, Engel, & Mooney, 1997). It is important that teachers be involved from the inception of the vision-building process if they are to share in and commit to putting the vision into practice (Conley, Dunlap, & Goldman, 1992). The principal, however, has the express responsibility for taking the lead in creating the shared vision, providing for its refinement, and keeping it alive by continually communicating it to all members of the school community.

An important step that a leader should take to facilitate the envisioning of a school's future is to learn everything about a school as it presently exists (Speck, 1999). Knowledge of the staff's norms for behavior, attitudes, and working relationships is important because these elements can all influence the change processes in a school. The following is the vision statement for the Hugo Newman College Preparatory School:

> P.S. 180 is a community of learners that is united in the belief that excellence in education is the only choice. We are dedicated to fostering literacy and developing English language arts and mathematical skills to become independent life-learners and problem

solvers. Towards this end we will develop an awareness within each student to view college as a viable and realistic goal.

The importance of vision at P.S. 180 is evident. It gives meaning to the work done by teachers, administrators, and students. It encourages team-work and reinforces the staff's press for improved teaching and learning. One of the major reasons that Principal McFarlane was able to galvanize his faculty to commit to working hard to achieve his school's goals was that he was adept at communicating to them a vision of where he wanted to take the school. This point was expressed over and over in our conver-sations with his teachers. At the same time, he understood that the vision for the school must be shared and was willing to include the desires and interests of the school community in creating the vision.

Strategies for Developing a Shared Vision Statement

Writing a vision statement is a process that unfolds over time as a result of discussion and reflection. Several writers (Barth, 1990; Chance & Grady, 1990; Speck, 1999) have suggested that a principal must have a per-sonal vision regarding how leadership will be provided for the school before working with the staff to develop a shared vision for the entire school. They point out that when a leader's personal vision has evolved, it is then possible to work with a staff to develop a vision that can be shared by all members of the school community.

In order to unleash their own personal vision, principals can address such questions as those suggested in Tips for Leaders 2.2.

Writing a Vision Statement: A Learning Strategy

Before the participants begin the actual work of "visioning," they must be at a readiness level to carry out the process. As is consistent with a constructivist approach, the development of the vision statement calls for new leadership roles to be assumed by teachers. It is important to provide members of the school community with staff development and profes-sional reading to prepare them for their roles (Wallace et al., 1997). To stim-ulate conversation about becoming a learning community and the school's vision, we generally recommend that reading material be provided on some of the topics suggested in Tips for Leaders 2.3. Other ideas can be found in the work of Wallace et al. (1997).

Writing a vision statement may take place over an extended period of time, and the participants will find it necessary to schedule a series of meetings to achieve consensus on the vision statement. The proposed

---

Tips for Leaders 2.2

Identifying Your Personal Vision for Your School

To uncover your personal vision for your school, reflect on the following questions:

- What does effective teaching look like?
- What knowledge and skills should teachers have to prepare students for their future?
- How can learning opportunities available to the teachers and students be maximized?
- How can teachers be guided to maintain a focus on learning outcomes for students?
- What roles should parents and the community assume in schools?
- What is my preferred leadership style?
- What does a learning community school look like?

SOURCE: Some of the ideas in this figure have been adapted from *The Principalship: Building a Learning Community*, by Marsha Speck and Debra A. Stollenwerk, © 1998. Reprinted by permission of Pearson Education.

visioning strategy is enormously meaningful for the building of community because, during the process,

1. The learning community attributes of collaboration, collegiality, reflective dialogue, and a focus on student learning are reinforced as part of the envisioning strategy.

2. The diverse values, beliefs, and attitudes about schooling and toward the school are uncovered and discussed in the open until consensus is achieved.

3. Members of the school community have a planned opportunity to engage in conversations to learn about their colleagues' views on teaching and learning.

4. Members of the school community have a planned opportunity to learn more about their school and its needs.

5. Teachers are afforded a chance to participate in team-building activities that serve to strengthen the learning community.

The principal and other leaders must be cognizant of the fact that the use of a collaborative development strategy does not necessarily result in

Tips for Leaders 2.3

Preparing Teachers and Community
Members for the Visioning Process

Help participants to participate in the vision-building process by
providing them with reading materials on such topics as

- Learning communities
- Standards movements in education
- Future skills needed by students in an culture of continuous
  change
- Achievement data for your school
- Research on teaching and learning
- Team building

the commitment of the entire school staff to the shared vision statement
(Smith & Piele, 1997). The leader's role is systematically to communicate
the vision to all of the school's stakeholders until it becomes part of the
expectations for the future.

How does a school community translate a shared vision into a vision
statement? There is no blueprint for accomplishing this, but the strategy we
use is described in Figure 2.2. It is one way of developing a vision statement,
and it may be adopted or modified to meet the needs of your school. It is
based on similar approaches (see the discussion in Wallace et al., 1997, Senge
et al., 2000, and Whitaker & Moses, 1991) to developing a vision statement
that can be found in the literature. A sample feedback form for facilitating
the visioning process is provided in Figure 2.3.

WHAT STRATEGIES CAN EDUCATIONAL LEADERS USE TO COMMUNICATE AND SUSTAIN THE VISION?

A number of writers (Fullan, 1991; Speck, 1999; Wallace et al., 1997) have
stressed that it is important for those in leadership positions to communicate
and assert commitment to their school's shared vision. The significance of a
school's shared vision has also been borne out by the Interstate School
Leaders Licensure Consortium ([ISLLC] 1996), a group of state agencies
and professional associations who jointly developed a set of six standards
for school leaders. ISLLC Standard #1 states,

Figure 2.2	Strategy for Developing a Vision Statement
Who	What
Principal	• Select an envisioning committee, including teachers, parents, students, and other members of the school community to guide the development of the shared vision statement. The principal serves on this committee. • Provide for the development of a shared vision by forming committees of grade-level or content-area teachers to take part in the process.
Envisioning Committee	• Develop a proposed list of questions and a feedback form that all committees can use to reflect on what they would like their school to look like in the future. • Draft a temporary time line for completing the committee's work.
Faculty Committee	• Reflect on their values and what they their want their school to look like in the future by discussing the envisioning questions. • Based on the discussion, generate and reach consensus on a list of indicators of the school they desire. • Prepare a vision statement; complete and submit the feedback form to the envisioning committee.
Envisioning Committee	• Pool and compare the indicators and vision statements developed by each committee. • Identify the indicators and statements on which consensus can be reached. • Formulate draft of a shared vision statement. • React to the draft and revise it if necessary. • Submit the draft to the faculty committee for review and feedback. • Use the feedback form to finalize the shared vision statement.

A school administrator is an educational leader who promotes the success of all students by facilitating the development, articulation, implementation, and stewardship of a vision of learning that is shared and supported by the school community. (p. 10)

Thus, the development of a shared vision statement is not the end of the visioning process. In fact, communication of the vision begins when a process is established for the entire school community to participate in its development. The principal then has the responsibility of keeping the vision alive (Deal & Peterson, 1994).

Figure 2.3   Feedback Form for Developing a Shared Vision

Feedback Form for Developing a Shared Vision

Directions: Each committee is to use this worksheet to develop a statement of a shared vision our school.

1. Reflect on and respond individually to the questions about your school.

2. Use your response to prepare a list of indicators of what you want your school to look like in the future.

3. Identify the indicators on which the committee can reach consensus.

4. Use the indicators on which you have reached consensus to draft a proposed shared vision statement describing how you see the school you would like.

Sample Reflection Questions:

1. What should our students and teachers be able to know and do?

2. What values should our students be encouraged to acquire?

3. What do we want our school to look like in the future?

4. What skills will our students require to prosper in the future?

5. What conditions in our school currently cause you some concern?

Indicators of the school we desire:

_____
_____
_____
_____
_____

Suggested shared vision statement(s):

_____
_____
_____
_____
_____

In our work, we have observed that the role of keeper of the vision is complex and that leaders of learning community schools must view it through a number of lenses. That is, effective leadership requires those in leadership positions to:

- Communicate and sustain a shared vision that has been collaboratively developed by the staff and the broader school community.
- Have a vision of how the learning community attributes are to be sustained.
- Nurture a shared vision of effective teaching, learning, and supervisory practices to maintain the focus on improving instructional practice (see Chapter 6).
- Recognize that individual members of the learning community may have personal visions that will guide some of their behaviors. This is especially true of teachers who characteristically develop deep-seated points of view about how their schools should operate based on their daily teaching and learning experiences. Principals must anticipate and be prepared to clearly address the issues that they surface during conversations about the learning community model.

Vision therefore plays a significant role in all aspects of the daily work life of a principal and its importance should be reflected in the principal's behavior. What are some of the leadership behaviors that contribute to maintaining the vision?

- We would suggest that every act of shared leadership reflect and communicate the principal's commitment to some aspect of a school's shared vision.
- To nurture the vision, leaders of learning communities should provide structured opportunities for learning community members to share their vision-related teaching and learning activities with one another and to collaboratively reflect on the beliefs they share in common.
- Teachers and other staff members should be afforded opportunities to make plans to translate the vision into practice (Starratt, 1995). Where appropriate, members of the broader school community should be invited to participate in the planning process.
- Leaders should talk about the school's vision and goals whenever possible (Deal & Peterson, 1994). Conversations about teaching and learning issues can take place at staff meetings, faculty meetings, parent-teacher meetings, and school assemblies, and during informal conversations with teachers.

- Leaders should ensure that the school's existing programs and practices are aligned with the values and direction implicit in the vision statement.
- The importance of the contributions made by teachers, staff, and community members in developing and carrying out the vision should be publicly acknowledged (Deal & Peterson, 1994).
- The vision statement should be reviewed each year with an eye toward revising it when the school community thinks it necessary (Bennis & Nanus, 1986).

In their classic work *The Leadership Paradox*, Deal and Peterson (1994) eloquently point out that public display is also an important way of communicating and maintaining a school's vision and values. Strategies for publicizing the vision that are suggested throughout the literature and that are now commonplace in many schools include displaying the vision statement in school entrances and other public areas, on memoranda and publicity materials, and on teacher-developed bulletin boards.

It should be noted that the ideas discussed above not only contribute to sustaining the vision, but are also important for community building. The behaviors that reinforce a school's vision also provide the school community with ongoing opportunities for learning. Although conversation helps to reinforce and deepen commitment to the vision, it cannot resolve the problems associated with transforming a school into a learning community. Elmore, Peterson, and McCarthey (1996) suggest that the new knowledge and ideas generated by teachers during structured conversations must be translated into instructional practice if ongoing student learning is to be fostered.

Conversations around vision take on a special meaning as our school communities become increasingly populated with families from many different backgrounds. Discussions that focus on "where we would like our school to go" can be the anchor that nurtures trust, understanding, and collaboration in school communities that serve children from diverse cultures. Leaders must be armed with an array of strategies that promote the development of trust.

HOW DO PRINCIPALS BUILD THE TRUST THAT CONTRIBUTES TO IMPROVED STUDENT ACHIEVEMENT?

Recently, the quality of working relationships among teachers and other members of a school community has been discussed as an important factor in successful school reform. In a large Illinois school district, it was found that where trust exists among principals, teachers, students, and parents, achievement scores on state tests were are either improved or improving. High performing schools were more often schools with higher levels of trust than the lowest performing schools. In schools reporting low levels of trust, reform efforts are likely to fail. The study linked trust with improved student outcomes (Bryk & Schneider, 2002).

Leadership Behaviors That Build Trust

Trust is an essential factor in building the high-quality relationships needed to foster collaboration in schools. Trust has been defined as "a group's generalized expectancy that the words, actions, and promises of another individual, group, or organization can be relied upon" (Hoy & Kupersmith, in Hoffman, Sabo, Bliss, & Hoy, 1994, p. 486). Where trust exists, teachers demonstrate a greater willingness to collaborate with principals on school reform strategies and curriculum issues and to reach out to parents. Principal McFarlane, as described in the vignette below, has consistently demonstrated the capacity to develop a trusting relationship with his teachers.

> *Dr. Peter McFarlane, principal of the Hugo Newman College Preparatory School has improved academic achievement in his school. At the time that he assumed the principalship, the school had been cited by the state as a low-achieving school for several years. One aspect of his leadership has been the building of trust with his teachers. McFarlane builds relationships through one-on-one conversations with his teachers. He is open to their ideas, candid and direct in conversations about school issues, and openly shares his opinions and values with his teachers.*

> *Principal McFarlane also builds trust with his teachers through a set of teacher-directed activities that he has structured. A series of committees have be set up through which teachers are empowered to make important decisions about literacy, technology, special education, and all other areas of the school's programs. Dr. McFarlane makes himself available to dialogue and exchange ideas with committee members. He listens carefully and respectfully to what they have to say and consistently follows up on their plans and recommendations. His focus is unfailingly on what is best for his students and the needs of his teachers. McFarlane also encourages his staff to maintain the same focus on what is of benefit to the students.*

Like McFarlane, principals who engender trust are consistent, fair, and respectful of the teachers, staff, parents, and students with whom they work. Principals promote trust in their schools by first fostering trust between themselves and their teachers. The process starts when a principal initiates shared leadership. What are the behaviors that contribute to the development of trust as a school move toward becoming a learning community? A list of behaviors that engender trust, culled from studies by Bryk and Schneider (2002), Barlow (2001), and Tschannen-Moran and Hoy (1998), and from our own observations in schools, is provided below.

Tips for Developing Trust

Principals build trust with teachers, parents, and members of the broader school community by doing the following:

- Talking about and inspiring others to work for a shared vision for the school.
- Always placing the interests of children first (Bryk & Schneider, 2002).
- Carrying out what he or she has agreed to do and acting in the interest of teachers (Tschannen-Moran & Hoy, 1998).
- Enthusiastically supporting teacher-initiated activities.
- Deferring to a team's decision when it differs from his or her preferences.
- Setting reasonable but challenging expectations for staff and students (Bryk & Schneider, 2002).
- Offering all teachers the opportunity to share the available resources and to participate in authentic learning opportunities (Bryk & Schneider, 2002).
- Encouraging and supporting teachers when they take risks.

Teachers build trust with principals, other teachers, parents, and members of the broader school community by doing the following:

- Working with other teachers to achieve school and district standards (Bryk & Schneider, 2002).
- Actively participating in learning activities, teamwork, and other school initiatives.
- Showing sensitivity and concern for their students.
- Trying out new instructional strategies.
- Courteously giving consideration to issues raised by parents and community members (Barlow, 2001).
- Being candid but collaborative in conversations about teaching and learning.

- Demonstrating the commitment and skill needed for students to achieve their grade level standards (Bryk & Schneider, 2002).

The above set of research-based behaviors is not exhaustive, but it does raise a number of points that leaders should be cognizant of if they are to foster trust in a school community. Obviously, trust stems from a set of behaviors and beliefs that must be practiced over time. Moreover, these behaviors and beliefs are all associated with the learning community characteristics of reflective dialogue, a focus on student learning, collaboration, shared values and norms, openness to improvement, and supportive leadership. This suggests that, to develop trust, those in leadership positions must create the conditions under which the characteristics of a learning community can take root. To provide the leadership needed for a school to become a learning community, they must be open to engaging in dialogue with the various constituencies in their school communities and consistently model trust-building behaviors. Obviously, they need effective communication skills to successfully engage in these behaviors. For further understanding of how trust develops in learning communities, we recommend Bryk and Schneider's (2002) work, *Trust in Schools: A Core Resource for Improvement*.

WHAT COMMUNICATION SKILLS DO LEADERS NEED TO SUCCESSFULLY LEAD LEARNING COMMUNITIES?

Let us return to Joseph Rios, the principal of School #5 in the Menlo School District.

> *Principal Rios has accepted our advice. His teachers now meet on a regular basis to dialogue about teaching and learning, and many teachers have begun to take on their roles as leaders and learners. However, he has noticed that too many teachers stand on the sidelines and do not actively or appropriately participate in the regularly scheduled conversations that are an integral part of workaday life at School #5. During his visits to other schools in the district, Principal Rios has learned that one of the keys to transforming the school's mission and vision into reality are the communication tools required to facilitate collaboration and reflection among the teachers and other staff members. What communication skills do the administrators and teachers at School #5 need to assume their roles as learners and leaders?*

Effective communication skills, which are essential for those in leadership positions, are at the heart of the learning activities that take place

Figure 2.4   Communication Skills to Promote Collaboration

Communication Skills Clusters	Communication Techniques
Sharing information	• Stating your position • Disclosing one's needs and feelings • Offering relevant information

Promoting Understanding	• Active listening
	  – Paraphrasing
	  – Asking for clarification
	  – Reflecting on others' feelings
	  – Summarizing
	  – Harmony between body and verbal language
	• Posing nonjudgmental questions
	• Offering support

SOURCE: These communication techniques have been adapted/reprinted from *The Handbook of Organization Development in Schools and College,* Schmuck and Runkel (1994). Copyright © Waveland Press. Reprinted by permission.

in learning community schools. Teachers need to communicate effectively to assume leadership roles and participate in learning activities with individuals and groups. Collaborative learning and relationships cannot take root and deepen in the absence of good communication skills. Based on relevant research (Fullan, 1991; Osterman, 1993; Schmuck & Runkel, 1994), we identify two clusters of skills (Figure 2.4), together with the associated techniques that promote effective interpersonal and group communication and collaboration. The skills clusters and techniques are discussed below.

Sharing Information

Communication between individuals and within collaborative groups is enhanced when individuals are adept at stating their positions, disclosing their needs and feelings, and offering relevant information. Attention should be given to the development of these skills when a school first commits to transforming into a learning community. When ideas and opinions are openly shared and supported with reliable facts, over time learning and trust among leaders and teachers can deepen (Schmuck & Runkel, 1994).

To promote sharing of information and collaborative learning, leaders in learning community schools should model the communication behaviors listed below as well as prompt their staff members to do the same:

- Consistently link shared information with improved student learning.
- Promote collegiality by expressing their support when they agree with comments made by team members.
- Honestly, clearly, and succinctly describe their points of view about the teaching and learning topics under discussion.
- Foster a collaborative climate by refraining from making judgmental statements about the ideas put forth by others.
- Strengthen interpersonal relationships and nurture trust by sharing their feelings so others may better understand their thinking.
- Include some time for reflection in group meetings as well as in one-on-one conversations.
- Enrich conversations with new facts and opinions that expand the dialogue and motivate others to join in the discussion.

Promoting Understanding

If students, teachers, and other members of a school community are to fully profit from their learning activities, promoting understanding must become a shared endeavor in their workday lives. In their one-on-one interactions as well as in structured group activities, understanding will be enhanced when they use the skills of (a) active listening, (b) posing nonjudgmental questions, and (c) offering support to colleagues. A great deal of attention has already been given to the importance of these techniques in the literature. Although they are presented as discrete skills, in practice they form an interrelated web of communicative behaviors that foster understanding. Leaders must model and nurture these skills so that the members of a learning community can come to recognize the unique role that each individual plays in communicating an understanding of the school's the vision, values, and teaching and learning practices. The communication acts that promote understanding, as briefly defined below, are compiled from the work of Schmuck and Runkel (1994) and our own observations in schools undergoing change.

Active listening, which is an attempt to gain a clear picture of what others are trying to communicate, is reflected in a number of behaviors. They include

- Rewording or paraphrasing a message to make certain you and others understand what is being said.
- Ensuring that everyone has an opportunity to participate in a discussion. As more team members begin to contribute to a group's conversations, it is more likely that shared understand will be achieved.
- Inquiring about the feelings and viewpoints of other team members. In our work, we have observed that teachers are more likely to see

themselves as valued members of the community when their colleagues give attention to and reflect on their ideas and feelings.

- Seeking more information when questions arise about the information being shared. Collegiality is fostered when teachers believe that their colleagues are interested in their opinions on instructional issues.
- Summarizing what has been learned during a discussion. Summarizing permits collaborative groups to recollect what they have learned in common and what agreed-upon actions are to be taken following collaborative conversations.

Nonjudgmental questions foster a climate in which trust can develop and conversation among team members can move ahead. We have all been in discussions where questions are posed that make teachers feel that they are being judged. The result is that dialogue is restricted and the development of collegial relationships where faculty members feel free to express themselves is made more difficult.

Genuine offers of support can deepen the relationships among the members of a school community. Volunteering to help other teachers reduces the sense of isolation that teachers typically experience. Statements of how and when assistance can be offered, such as, "I would be glad to work with you and your students on Thursday afternoon," promote collegiality and contribute to the sense of community in schools.

In additional to modeling the above-listed behaviors, when necessary, principals should provide teachers with training, as effective communication is a powerful and fundamental tool for building community. Extensive information, training activities, and exercises for practicing the skills can be found in Schmuck and Runkel's *Handbook of Organization Development in Schools and Colleges* (1994).

Finally, it is critically important that those in leadership positions follow up on what they have agreed to do in meetings. We view follow-up behavior as a form of communication. Leaders who consistently follow up communicate that they are trustworthy, respectful of their teachers, and genuinely support the collaborative processes that are the glue of learning community schools. Additionally, effective communication helps to smooth the road to carrying out the process of change in schools.

WHAT DO LEADERS NEED TO KNOW ABOUT THE CHANGE PROCESS?

Bringing about change in any school has invariably proven to be an elusive endeavor. The transformation of a school into a learning community requires teachers and administrators to engage in conversations that may

---

Tips for Leaders 2.4

Listening Skills Survey

Use the communication skill clusters in Figure 2.4 to identify the communication techniques by staff members at a meeting. Which skills do they use well? Which skills do they fail to use? If needed, provide them with a workshop on communication skills to improve the quality of their conversations.

---

question (a) their instructional practices, (b) their mental models, and (c) the school's structures.

Questioning Instructional Practices

In learning communities, teachers no longer plan for and carry out instruction in isolation from one another. They question their instructional practices by collaboratively discussing and making decisions about teaching and learning issues. The outcome is discovery of original ways of resolving instructional issues.

Questioning Mental Models

Senge (1990) describes *mental models* as "deeply ingrained assumptions, generalizations, or even pictures or images that influence how we understand the world and how we take action" (p. 8). As those in leadership positions attempt to bring about change, they must be aware of the effect these mental models have on faculty, on staff, and on teaching and learning. For example, consider the Menlo School District:

- Many teachers in the Menlo School District assume that the best way to provide instruction is to group students in self-contained classrooms based on their achievement scores. This mental model is a barrier to the teachers taking a serious look at other ways of providing instruction for students.

- Jack Carson, Menlo's Director of Curriculum, assumes that his committee of district coordinators will make the best decisions about instructional issues for all of Menlo's schools. The mental model that he holds can have a significant impact on what is to be taught, how it is to be taught, and on the learning outcomes for students.

Tips for Leaders 2.5

Learn About Your Mental Models

The mental models that we hold about people or institutions restrict us to behaving and thinking in our usual manner.

- Think about a pressing issue(s) that poses a challenge for your role as a leader in your school.
- Identify the mental model that guides your behavior in the face of the challenge
- How does this mental model affect your behavior with teachers, students, or supervisors?

It is therefore important for educational leaders to be cognizant of the mental models held by individuals in their school community and by the school community as a whole. If change is to occur, educators must systematically examine their perceptions about schooling, consider their expectations for students, and find new ways of working together to bring about change in their schools (Senge et al. 2000).

Questioning the School's Structures

Many of the old structures in schools, such as structures for making decisions about curriculum and instruction, strategies for resolving schoolwide problems, and providing leadership, will have to be examined and changed. These structures often block efforts to bring about the changes that promote the shift to a collaborative culture and the building of community (Senge et al., 2000).

The Principal's Role

If the principal, who is charged with steering the school through the change, is unwilling to share leadership with teachers, meaningful and lasting reform cannot be achieved. Because teachers must eventually carry out any proposed changes, it is important that they clearly see the fit between their new roles as leaders and learners and the teaching and learning responsibilities that constitute their everyday work lives.

Tips for Leaders 2.6

The Principal's Role in Managing the Transition to a Learning Community

- Change requires leadership. The principal has to take charge by educating and empowering teacher leaders and serving as an advocate for the reform effort (Pokorny, 1997; Sparks, 1993).
- Acquire a deep understanding of the change process and the nature of a learning community.
- Demonstrate your commitment to the learning community attributes of collective learning, collegiality, collaboration and shared leadership by

  - Setting understandable goals and using a committee/team approach to ensure that all members of the community can participate in the planning process (Sparks, 1993).
  - Sharing power with teachers and others to provide for a diversity of ideas and promote commitment to the changes (Sarason, 1990; Sparks, 1993).
  - Modeling commitment to collegial learning by frequently sharing and seeking information from members of the school community.

- Remember that the pace of and path to change differs for each individual. Be patient.
- Remember that individuals must change if the school is to change. Know beliefs, ideas, and objections— emotional and intellectual—of your teachers (Hall & Hord, 2001).
- Recognize the efforts made by individuals as they work to transition into a learning community.
- Confront resisters by publicly and privately defending the school's mission and vision.

Michael Fullan (1993) provides several lessons about change that we offer for the consideration of principals. Change, which is filled with a lack of certainty about the future, does not occur simply because it has been mandated. Nevertheless, administrators, as well as teachers, can learn by confronting the problems they meet as they go through the process. A set of tips that have been culled from the literature and that can assist leaders in managing change are provided in Tips for Leaders 2.6.

Information Online 2.1

The report *Hope for Urban Education: A Study of Nine High Performing High-Poverty Urban Elementary Schools* (Charles A. Dana Center, University of Texas at Austin, 1999), available at http://www.ed.gov/pubs/urbanhope/ index.html, includes nine case studies that describe the schools and sets out to explain how they transformed themselves into high-achieving schools. Read three of the case studies to identify how the change processes in the school reflect Sarason's three underlying principles about change.

We have found time and time again that facilitating change is often hampered because people in schools tend to behave in ways that delay progress as they gradually regress to their customary way of functioning. To bring about change, leaders must be prepared to (1) involve all members of the school community, both insiders and outsiders, (2) improve conditions for teaching and learning, and (3) share power (Sarason, in Speck, 1999).

HOW DO YOU BEGIN THE PROCESS OF BUILDING A LEARNING COMMUNITY?

We cannot provide a cookbook describing how to initiate the transformation of your school into a learning community. Every school is different, every faculty is different, and the shift to a culture that reflects the learning community characteristics cannot be presented in the form of a recipe. The leadership behaviors that contribute to school change cannot be presented as a quantifiable sequence of activities. We do, however, recommend that principals respect the following steps, which are a summary of many of the strategies provided throughout the book:

1. Be armed with a deep knowledge of the learning community characteristics and the strategies for fostering their development (Speck, 1999).

2. Acquire in-depth knowledge of the school's history and strengths and of the available opportunities and constraints that may have an impact on the change process.

3. Take every opportunity to educate your staff and the broader school community about the characteristics of learning communities.

4. Obtain the support of the district leadership for your planned change and identify the resources needed to carry out the change.

5. Gain your teachers trust by finding ways of sharing your leadership with them (Hord, 1997).

6. Listen to your teachers and always follow up on what you hear and promise to do.

7. Provide the structures necessary for learning (e.g., team meetings, grade-level meetings, study groups, etc.) and look for other opportunities for your teachers to collaborate around meaningful teaching and learning issues (Hord, 1997).

8. Demonstrate the value you place on learning by actively participating in learning activities with the teachers.

9. Exhibit strong and consistent leadership (Barth, 1990).

10. Consistently focus on the outcomes of instruction (DuFour & Eaker, 1998).

CONCLUSION

Teachers in learning communities must have the opportunity to work, plan, and learn together around instructional issues. Time must be structured to ensure that collaboration becomes an important part of their school day and the school week.

The change to a learning community requires a shift from a culture of isolation to a culture of conversation; from a focus on teaching students to a focus on reciprocal teaching and learning by all members of the school community; and from leadership by a few individuals to leadership that is embedded in and shared by all members of the school community. To accomplish this, principals must work with teacher and the wider school community to building a shared vision and mission for their school, communicate the vision, acquire and use communication skills that foster collaboration and commitment, plan and facilitate the change process, promote the development of teachers as collaborative leaders and learners, and ensure sustained academic achievement.

ACTIVITIES

1. Develop a survey instrument to gather information on how those in formal leadership positions foster collaboration among teachers. Survey the building-level administrators in your district. Use the results of the study to improve teacher collaboration in your school.
2. Visit a learning community school. Interview several teachers about the nature of the principal's leadership behaviors.
3. Talk to several teachers to identify the mental models that drive instruction in your school. What are the consequences of these models for the delivery of instruction?
4. Interview the principal and three teachers in your school about the change process. Collect information on the following:

   a. In what ways does the school need to change?

   b. What are the barriers to change in the school?

   c. Who should be involved in the change process and what should be the nature of their involvement?

   d. Did you identify any discrepancies in the answers of the teachers and the principal? If so, what are the implications of these differences for the change process?

NOTES

1. The information on facilitative leadership was adapted from "Ten Propositions for Facilitative Leadership," by Conley and Goldman (1994, pp. 237–262). Copyright © by Corwin Press. Adapted by permission of Corwin Press.

2. Abstracted from *Building Leadership Capacity in Schools,* by Lambert (1998). Copyright © Association for Supervising and Curriculum Development (www.ascd.org). Reprinted with permission from ASCD. All rights reserved.

3 Learning Through Ongoing Professional Development

PREVIEW OF THE CHAPTER

In the professional learning community, everyone is a learner. It is an environment in which staff members continuously explore new ideas and seek to improve their practice in order to effect increased student achievement. Ongoing professional development is vital to the learning community and has become even more important in the face of curriculum standards and increased accountability for teachers and for schools. This chapter examines principles, standards, and strategies for nurturing effective professional development. It addresses the following questions:

- What are the guiding principles for professional development in learning communities?
- What strategies meet the needs of adults as learners?
- How can we find enough time for professional development?
- How do we assess the effectiveness of professional development?
- How do we get started with professional development?

WHAT ARE THE GUIDING PRINCIPLES FOR PROFESSIONAL DEVELOPMENT IN LEARNING COMMUNITIES?

Pat Martin, a new teacher in the Menlo School District, is talking with one of his friends who started teaching in another district the same month he started in Menlo. His friend is complaining about the staff development programs in her school.

"They are so boring. Some so-called expert comes in and talks at us. Every month, it's somebody else with a different topic. The topics have nothing to do with what we're really teaching or the issues we're concerned about. In fact, they don't know or care what we are doing in our classrooms; they just want to push the latest educational model and spout the latest buzzwords. The principal and the superintendent do all the deciding and the teachers never get to say what we really want."

"It's very different in Menlo," Pat says. "We teachers have a big say in our professional development. We work together and learn together. Staff development seems like part of the job. You can hardly tell them apart. Just the other day we had a great session looking at our students' work in relation to curriculum standards. We learned so much from each other. In fact, teachers lead a lot of the staff development in Menlo. I told you, you should have come to Menlo. You would have had more of a say in your own professional development."

This conversation between Pat, who works in a school on its way to becoming a learning community, and his friend, who does not, points out some of the differences in professional development in the two settings. Several principles guide staff development in learning communities. First of all, the primary focus of professional development is student outcomes: It is results driven and focused on curriculum and standards (Guskey, 2000; Joyce & Showers, 1988; Sparks & Hirsh 1997). The process of professional growth in the learning community is job embedded, collaborative, site based, and ongoing (Bull & Buechler, 1996). Teachers in the learning community take more responsibility for their own professional growth (Sparks & Hirsh, 1997). Finally, successful professional development is conducted in accordance with the high standards set by the profession (DuFour & Eaker, 1998; National Staff Development Council [NSDC], 2001). Although in real situations these elements are intertwined, they will be examined separately in the following sections.

Improved Student Outcomes

Ultimately, the bottom line for effective professional development is improved student achievement (Joyce & Showers, 1988; Sparks & Hirsh, 1997). Successful staff development encourages teachers to look at the actual results they are getting with students and change their practice if these results are not what they want. It is focused on ensuring that all children learn (NSDC, 2001). It encourages educators to concentrate on the relationship between their teaching and the students' achievement and to look at what works and what does not. Teachers should be willing to change their approaches if their students are not learning.

A teacher in a school of which one of the authors was principal was a great example of this attitude. She kept a sign over her door that said, "If they don't learn the way I teach, I'll teach the way they learn." To her, this was much more than a sign: It was her commitment. Her strong dedication to student learning came through in her teaching and she was one of the best teachers in the school. Year after year, her students all achieved very well, no matter what they had done in other classes. Good professional development should encourage this kind of spirit in all teachers.

Curriculum Standards

In today's world, student achievement is measured in large part by how well the curriculum standards are met. Consequently, professional development must be linked to these standards (DuFour & Eaker, 1998). The standards can provide a unifying theme for staff development over several years. An example of this is the experience one of the authors had working with curriculum standards in school districts for several years.

When the state curriculum standards first came out, much of the author's work as a consultant was helping schools become aware of and familiar with them. Then we guided teachers in examining what these standards looked like when applied to their own classrooms, even if they were not teaching at one of the grade levels being tested. We helped them look at their own curriculum guides in relation to the standards and refine them or design new ones if necessary. As schools and teachers have become more sophisticated about the standards, our work evolved into facilitating as teachers develop themes, specific lessons, assessment procedures, and report cards incorporating the standards. They are also reexamining their texts and other materials through this lens. Throughout the years, we have used collaboration, group processes, discussion, teacher research, and reflection focused on the standards. It has been exhilarating to see the intellectual excitement that is stimulated by collegial interaction around day-to-day instructional matters in their own classrooms. Based on our experience with the faculties of many schools, we agree with Carr and Harris (2001) that professional development guided by a clear vision of learning gives teachers the chance to expand their knowledge, strengthen their skills, take on leadership, and build a learning community.

If they are to help students master content, teachers themselves must be highly competent in the disciplines they teach. Good staff development helps to expand teachers' knowledge of the curriculum content. It focuses both on what students learn and how they learn. Although general teaching strategies are still included, staff development in the learning community is increasingly focused on content and pedagogy for specific disciplines, such as language arts, math, or science (Sparks & Hirsh, 1997). As more states establish curriculum standards, staff development must be increasingly linked to them. Suggested strategies based on our own experiences and the literature relating to curriculum standards follow.

Strategies

- Keep the curriculum goals and standards posted in the faculty room and school lobby as a constant reminder. We have observed that parents as well as staff take note of them.
- Engage the faculty in curriculum mapping individually (Jacobs, 1997), then by grade level, and then the whole school. This helps the staff become aware of what is actually being taught in the school, and we have found it to be a powerful tool for enhancing the sense of community.
- Have teachers work in teams to examine student assessment results to identify instructional strengths and weaknesses and to plan strategies for improving the school's achievement level.
- Hold workshops in which teachers demonstrate strategies related to curriculum standards that really work. Focus on a particular discipline and have teachers bring related student products. Allow ample time for discussion.
- Document outstanding lessons related to standards and disperse them to all staff members. They may be written up or videotaped.
- Conduct a series of discussions on curriculum standards ranging from familiarity with them to using them in assessment procedures and report cards.

Collaborative Professional Development

An important characteristic of professional development in the learning community is that it is collaborative (DuFour & Eaker, 1998; Hord, 1997). As

Pat Martin pointed out in the opening vignette, teachers learn together and learn from each other. A more expanded perspective is possible when the diverse opinions and experiences of community members are shared. Collaborative activities should include teachers of special needs students as well as mainstream teachers. The synergy that results as teachers interact is stimulating and moves the community forward. Collaborative approaches are discussed in more detail in Chapters 4 through 8 of this book.

Job-Embedded Professional Development

Effective professional development and day-to-day practice are inextricably bonded in the learning community. Staff development is not just an irrelevant activity added on at the end of the day: It is part of the job (Wood & McQuarrie, 1999). As Pat said in the opening vignette, "You can hardly tell them apart." Professional development is more meaningful and more productive when it addresses the problems and situations faced by teachers on a day-to-day basis (Sparks & Hirsh, 1997). Job-embedded professional development strategies are associated with the characteristics of a learning community in that they are collaborative and offer opportunity for conversation, reflection, and inquiry (see Figure 3.1). They are also in accord with the principle that adult learners respond best when dealing with real-life situations and problems. In this book, job-embedded learning is considered to be the fundamental approach to the professional development of teachers and the building of learning communities. Accordingly, job-embedded learning professional development strategies in which teachers, administrators, and other staff collaborate and learn together as they engage in their daily work will be the focus of the chapters to follow. Specific approaches for job-linked professional growth, such as looking at student work, mentoring, forming study groups, conducting school walk-throughs, and developing professional portfolios, are discussed in the upcoming chapters.

School-Based Professional Development

Staff development has undergone a shift over the years. Rather than being dominated by the district, there is now more emphasis on school-based planning and implementation (Sparks & Hirsh, 1997). (This, however, does not mean that the district no longer has a beneficial role in staff development.) Even when staff development emanates from the district, individual schools should have input so that the needs of their particular students and the unique culture of the school are taken into account.

On-site staff development offers the opportunity for staff members to visit one another's classrooms, meet frequently, discuss things both informally and formally, and share perspectives about the same students. In a

Figure 3.1	Activities for Job-Embedded Professional Development

1. Observe other teachers teach.
2. Plan lessons and units with other teachers.
3. Give and receive feedback on instructional behaviors from peers.
4. Conduct action research projects.
5. Mentor new teachers.
6. Coach one another.
7. Keep a reflective log.
8. Develop and maintain a professional portfolio.
9. Look at student work together.
10. Become part of a study group.

site-based approach, it is easier to make the necessary changes in the culture of the school to move it toward becoming a learning community than when control emanates solely from the central office. Although the school vision should be in accord with the district vision, the school should be able to develop approaches that meet the needs of it own population and unique culture. As an example of this, we have worked with schools as they

- Conducted their own needs assessment, collected data about their students, and articulated their vision in accordance with the district vision.
- Developed their own action plans and techniques for assessing their effectiveness.
- Conducted staffwide activities focused on identified issues within the school. For example, teachers have shared video-clips of their classes at work, and brought in student products to discuss with one another. Teachers of upper grades have sat through lessons and taken tests as students do. This helped the teachers to more fully understand the difficulties their students might have. The teachers then reflected collaboratively on the experience with the aim of improving instruction and testing procedures and outcomes.

Activities like these within the individual schools encourage teacher growth and foster the community of learners.

Ongoing Professional Development

Professional development in the learning community is continuous. It is not a one-shot or fragmented approach, such as Pat's friend experienced.

There is ongoing inquiry, experimentation, and assessment as teachers seek to increase their effectiveness (Barth, 1990; Speck, 1999). Staff development has greater impact when it continues in the school over a period of years as opposed to one or two sessions. Learning experiences are cumulative and rigorous. In addition to being continuous for the learning community as a whole, it is ongoing for individual teachers throughout their careers, from the newly inducted teacher to the veteran staff member. The literature and our own experience suggest the following strategies for fostering continuity.

Strategies

- Develop long-range and short-range plans for staff development for the learning community. Student achievement should always be foremost in these plans.
- Plan staff development around a unifying theme or goal rather than offering many unrelated, fragmented topics.
- Build new learning experiences on what has gone before.
- Do a yearly assessment of progress toward the goals of the learning community, even for multiyear plans.
- Teachers should develop their individual professional growth plans on an ongoing basis and check their own progress annually.

Teacher Responsibility

An important aspect of professional development in the learning community is that teachers plan their own professional growth individually or collectively (Sparks & Hirsh, 1997). This by no means takes the onus off the school or district in terms of providing direction, resources, and time for teacher growth. It simply means that the teachers, individually and in collaboration with colleagues, should have a say in the content and form of their own professional development, as Pat Martin experienced in Menlo.

Furthermore, teachers in learning communities lead many staff development activities themselves rather than outside consultants. Teachers are recognized as experts and sometimes are more effective than outside consultants. One example of this occurred in a school where one of the authors was principal. The author who served as a principal and her staff wanted to have more emphasis on hands-on experiences in math for young children. The district sent experts in math who came and shared many good ideas. But it was not until we asked one of our own teachers to run a workshop for the rest of the faculty that things really took off. She brought many examples of work from her own classroom. Because these were essentially the same children they were working with, the other teachers knew that these activities would work with their own classes. They could go to her room and see her children actually working at these activities. They could ask her questions in the faculty room at lunch. The teacher who ran the workshops found it beneficial, too. She enjoyed sharing ideas, and she said that planning for the workshops helped her to articulate more clearly for herself why she did what she did and stimulated her to observe her students more closely for their reactions to the instruction.

Strategies

- Individual teachers may align their own professional development with improved student achievement just as schools and districts do. Instruments have been designed to help teachers with this (Richardson, 2002). The steps incorporated in these tools include

  1. Collecting and analyzing data about the students, focusing on three or four goals that relate to your school or district goals.
  2. Thinking about the reasons for poor performance and what you can do for improvement.
  3. Creating an action plan with goals for yourself and developing specific activities for each of these goals.

- Tap the expertise of teachers on the faculty. Encourage them to run workshops for their colleagues, sharing ideas that have worked successfully in their own classrooms.
- Encourage teachers to serve on committees to plan, implement, and evaluate staff development programs for their schools and districts.

Standards for Professional Development

Effective professional development is conducted in accordance with the standards of the profession. There are several sets of standards for professional development in education. One example is that of the NSDC (2001). These standards emphasize that staff development should improve the learning of all children. They address the context, process, and content of professional improvement and incorporate many of the principles already discussed.

The context standards encourage learning communities to have goals linked to those of the school and the district. They stress the need for leaders to promote ongoing improvement and resources to support adult learning.

```
┌─────────────────────────────────────────────────────────┐
│                                                         │
│                  Tips for Leaders 3.1                   │
│                                                         │
│                Assessing Staff Development              │
│                                                         │
│  Have the staff study the NSDC standards for profes-    │
│  sional development and collaboratively develop indi-   │
│  cators for each standard. Assess the school's staff    │
│  development program using these indicators. The NSDC   │
│  publishes the Journal of Staff Development, which has  │
│  many helpful articles on professional development for  │
│  educators. Their Website is http://www.nsdc.org.       │
│                                                         │
└─────────────────────────────────────────────────────────┘
```

The process standards emphasize that staff development should be research based. It should be driven by student data and use multiple sources of information for evaluation. It utilizes knowledge about learning and promotes collaboration.

Content standards promote equity, instructional quality, and family involvement. Effective staff development guides educators in understanding all students and having high expectations for them. It strengthens educators' knowledge of content research-based instructional strategies and various assessment procedures. It gives educators the knowledge and skills to engage families and other stakeholders.

WHAT STRATEGIES MEET THE NEEDS OF ADULTS AS LEARNERS?

Brain Research

In recent years, there has been extensive research in neuroscience resulting in a flurry of publications about the brain, how it works, and implications for instruction (Jensen, 1998; Shore, 1997; Sousa, 2001a, 2001b, 2002; Wolfe, 2001). According to Wolfe (2001), this new knowledge is due in part to advanced technology, which enables us to see the brain in action as opposed to studying the parts of the brain during an autopsy. In addition to enhancing our understanding of the brain, many of these works offer specific suggestions for brain-compatible instructional strategies. Although what we do not know still outstrips our knowledge about the brain, some of the findings validate many of the strategies that good teachers have used all along, such as interactive approaches and hands-on

---

Tips for Leaders 3.2

Leadership and the Brain

For a discussion of leadership in light of the emerging knowledge about the brain, see the work of Dickman and Stanford-Blair (2002).

---

learning. One of the exciting findings is that the brain's capacity to learn is limitless. In opposition to old theories that stated that the older brain cannot learn and that brain function deteriorates in old age, this means that learning can be lifelong. This gives added support to the concept of a community of learners where the adults as well as youngsters are continuously learning.

Needs of Adult Learners

Adults learn somewhat differently from children. Andragogical theories (as opposed to pedagogical theories) inform us about adults' motivation to learn, the process of adult learning, and strategies that are most effective for adult learners (Knowles, Holton, & Swanson, 1998). According to these theories, adults are more ready to learn if they have a practical use for the knowledge and think it will benefit them in real life. They usually learn for a specific reason rather than just for the love of learning. Preserving self-esteem and pleasure are other motivating factors for adult learners.

The works of Mitchell (1998) and Knowles et al. (1998) provide the following insights about the learning process for adults. Adult learners are more self-reliant than children are and resist others dictating to them what they should learn. They prefer to be in charge of their own learning. They need to connect new concepts to what they already know in order to make use of new ideas. They learn best when the new concepts and skills are related to real-life circumstances. This is one reason that job-embedded staff development is so effective. Adults need follow-up support, such as coaching, to help them transfer their new skills into everyday practice. They tend to take fewer risks than children do for fear of affecting their self-esteem. Because of the number and diversity of experiences they have had, adult groups are much more heterogeneous than children's groups.

Tips for Leaders 3.3

Handling Reluctant Learners

Adults do not learn much if they are reluctant. One effective way of handling teachers who are resistant to new ideas is to let them express their feelings. Once you know what the problem is, you are better able to deal with it. Empathize with them and show them how the new knowledge or skills will be of practical use to them in their daily classroom practice.

Learning is hindered when the aforementioned conditions are not met. Other obstacles include resistance to change, fear of appearing ignorant or incompetent, and fear of reprimands by superiors.

The knowledge about adult learning informs professional development in learning communities and strongly supports job-linked approaches. It points out the appropriateness of coaching, mentoring, and other ongoing follow-up strategies. Additional tips culled from our own professional knowledge base and the literature follow.

Strategies

- Make learning both an active and an interactive process.
- Provide hands-on, concrete experiences and real-life situations.
- Employ novelty, but also connect to the adult learners' prior experiences and knowledge.
- Give them opportunities to apply the new knowledge to what they already know or have experienced.
- Be aware of the diversity in an adult group. Use a variety of approaches to accommodate different learning styles and experiences and use examples that reflect the diversity in the group composition.
- Use small group activities through which learners have the opportunity to reflect, analyze, and practice what they have learned.
- Provide coaching, technical assistance, feedback, or other follow-up support as part of the training.
- Give adult learners as much control as possible over what they learn, how they learn, and other aspects of the learning experience.

Keep in mind these points regarding adult learners, as you read the following examples of techniques we have used over the years as consultants in staff development in our own schools, and in training graduate students. These activities facilitate learning and help to build a sense of community among the participants. We are not sure where the following activities originated, but we have found them to be effective as part of our training programs.

Carousel. This activity provides the opportunity for small groups to share ideas with one another and add ideas to one another's work. After working in small groups on a particular issue or topic, each group lists their ideas on newsprint sheets, which are posted in different areas around the room. Each group stands by the paper containing its own ideas, and then rotates on signal to the next group's work, where they may add ideas with markers they take with them. Rotation continues until all groups are back to their starting points. Each group can then read, reflect, and discuss the ideas that have been added to their original sheets. In addition to seeing all of the ideas that have been generated by the other groups, we have found that people enjoy getting up and moving around.

Draw It. This activity taps the creative side of participants. Working in small groups, they graphically represent the concept being presented or their feeling on the topic using newsprint and markers. They may use humor and utilize symbolism if they wish. Being artistic, however, is not necessary. One example we use as a discussion starter is to draw a picture of the perfect teacher. When all of the groups have finished their pictures, they post them and explain them. Our experience has been that groups have great fun with this approach once they realize they do not have to be artists. The illustrations stimulate great discussion, and sometimes the results are absolutely hilarious.

Headlines. We use this approach to envision conditions, as when developing an action plan, or to review concepts previously learned in a novel way. Working in small groups with newsprint and markers, participants create headlines about either concepts already learned or what could occur if the vision were realized. Discussion occurs in the small groups as they develop the headlines and again in the whole group as the small groups share their headlines.

Think, Pair, Share. This activity gives learners the opportunity to reflect on a concept being presented individually, in pairs, and then with the whole group. Participants are asked to reflect individually on the issue presented for one minute, and then to discuss it with a partner, each partner having one minute to share. Then, they share ideas with the whole group. We have found that people who are shy about talking to the whole group are quite comfortable talking in pairs. The bolder of the two may present their ideas to the whole group.

We recommend that leaders develop a large repertoire of activities to use with adults so that a variety of techniques may be used depending on the project. One of the authors worked with a newly organized school to help it develop its vision, mission, and objectives using a wide array of interactive strategies. At the end of the session, several teachers came up to say that they had dreaded coming because they thought it would be boring. Instead, they had had so much fun that they were sorry the sessions were over. Moreover, they had a final product they could be proud of and they got to know their new colleagues much better in the process. Activities suitable for adult learners in the professional learning community may be found in the literature in such works as Johnson and Johnson (2000), Schmuck and Runkel (1994), and Wald and Castleberry (2000).

HOW CAN WE FIND ENOUGH TIME FOR PROFESSIONAL DEVELOPMENT?

Time is an element that always seems to be in short supply in schools. Yet it is an important consideration, both in terms of when professional development takes place and how long it should last.

Even though effective professional development is embedded in the job, there still has to be time for teachers to meet, discuss, and work together. Many faculties have come up with solutions to this problem. Some examples for dealing with time constraints culled from our own experiences, from schools with which we have worked, and from the literature include

- Early release days for students. Some districts do this as often as once a week; others just once or twice a year.

- Scheduling common planning time, so that teams may work together.

- Coverage by specialists. The art, music, and other special teachers may cover classes so that a team of teachers may meet.

- Coverage by substitutes for a half day or whole day. Districts that are large enough may have a "School on Wheels," (Bull & Buechler, 1996), a cadre of specially trained substitutes with their own principal who travel to schools throughout the district to release the teachers for professional development.

- Meetings before school opens.

- Meetings after school closes.

- Changing the focus of the regular faculty meeting to include collaborative professional development activities.

- Closing schools on professional development days.

- Paid summer programs.

- Adding paid days to the school year for the staff earmarked for professional development.

- Having the staff members go on a retreat. Such a retreat could also include parents, depending on its purpose.

- Having large group activities for students, such as video viewing, covered by a minimum of staff while teams of teachers meet. One school came up with a creative approach called the "Friday Forums" (Hudson, 2002) that engages students as well as teachers and requires no additional time at the end of the day and no closing of school. Periodically, students go to special classes of their choice led by volunteers and organized by a part-time coordinator. This arrangement has many advantages. Students get to pursue their interests while teachers carry out their professional learning activities. Furthermore, there is no need for parents to find childcare, since there is no closing of school or shortening of the day.[1]

HOW MAY WE ASSESS THE EFFECTIVENESS OF PROFESSIONAL DEVELOPMENT?

It is just as important to assess professional development as it is to assess the instructional program for students. As Sparks and Hirsh (1997) point out, "Results driven education for students requires results driven staff development for educators" (p. 5). Ultimately, the way to find out whether professional development is really working is to determine whether there has been any impact on student performance, although other factors may also be taken into consideration. Evaluation helps to determine if the program is meeting the learning community's objective and points the way to continuous improvement.

Guidelines for Evaluating Staff Development Programs

Several principles for evaluating professional development programs culled from the literature (Guskey, 2000, 2002; Mullins, 1994) and our own experiences are offered below.

Information Online 3.1

The NSDC and Eisenhower National Clearinghouse for Mathematics and Science Education has a CD-ROM, *By your Own Design: A Teacher's Professional Learning Guide,* that helps teachers in developing and evaluating professional learning plans. It can be ordered from the NSDC Website, http://www.nsdc.org/bookstore.htm.

- Design the evaluation process before the professional development begins. Do not wait until the program has started before figuring out how to evaluate it.

- Evaluation should be ongoing. It should begin in the initial stages of the program and continue after its close. This way, information is available during the implementation process so that adjustments may be made if necessary.

- The bottom line of professional development is improved student learning. Therefore, the program evaluation should be based on its impact on students as well as on teachers. We want to know the impact of staff development on student outcomes, not just whether the teachers were satisfied or entertained.

- Evidence should be collected from many sources, such as student test scores and portfolios, teacher comments, surveys, interviews, and observations (Joyce & Showers, 1988). Guskey (2000, 2002) observes that there are five important levels of evaluation: (1) participants' reactions, (2) participants' learning, (3) organizational support and change, (4) the extent to which participants use the new concepts and skills, and (5) impact on student learning.

- Evaluation of the professional development program should be done by people familiar with staff development and committed to the task.

Strategies

Guskey (2000) offers many other suggestions for the evaluation process, which include the five levels mentioned above. Some of them are summarized below by permission of Corwin Press:

- Define the goals and objectives of the staff development program. They should be in accord with the mission of the school and should include improved student achievement as the ultimate goal.
- Decide how you are going to evaluate professional development and what evidence you will need, and then collect your baseline data. These may be student test scores, pre-questionnaires for the participants, or other information depending on the nature of the program and what is being evaluated.
- Collect participant comments and document what they have learned. Comments and immediate reactions are usually collected at the conclusion of the staff development session; it takes longer to get evidence of the participants' actual learning. Pre- and post-questionnaires focused on the content of the training, participant portfolios, and reflections are some ways of getting this information.
- Document evidence of organizational support and change. This information has to be gathered over time after the program ends through such items as district and school records, participants' portfolios, and questionnaires.
- Find out if the participants use the knowledge and skills in the classroom. This may be gathered through direct observations, video and audiotapes, participants' portfolios, and reflections.
- Gather evidence of student learning outcomes, including test scores, student portfolios, and other forms of documentation.
- Analyze all of the data, summarize, and make recommendations in a report.
- Once these steps are completed, adjustments should be made and new plans developed. It is important to recognize that, in a professional learning community, evaluation of professional development must be an ongoing process.

HOW DO WE GET STARTED WITH PROFESSIONAL DEVELOPMENT?

Teachers in the learning community have a greater role in planning and implementing these programs. They conduct the training and share their experiences. Some form school improvement committees, which take the planning of professional development as one of their responsibilities. The important thing to remember is that in a professional learning community, everyone is a learner. Staff training might include noncertified staff, such as aides, teaching assistants, and even parents. Other efforts may be directed

---

Tips for Leaders 3.4

Staff Development for New Teachers

Be sure to have a strong professional development program for new teachers. There should be a special orientation for them at the beginning of the year and ongoing mentoring throughout the year. Make sure they are included in faculty study groups as well.

---

only to new teachers. Financial and other resources are needed for effective professional development. These include funds for paying teachers for time spent outside of their contract time, the cost of materials and equipment needed for the training, travel expenses, and payment for consultants.

What Works?

Researchers who looked at effective professional development found that appropriate duration of training, a focus on subject matter content, and the use of active learning strategies are very important characteristics (Birman, Desimone, Porter, & Garet, 2000). They also found that when several teachers from the same grade or department take training together (collective participation), the training is more effective. They further discovered that when the staff development is related to other training, connects to day-to-day activities, and supports the curriculum standards, it is more likely to be successful.[2]

Much of the staff development today recognizes the expertise of staff members and the ability of teachers to inquire and conduct research on their own. But there are still times when an outside consultant may be called, as when expertise in a certain area is required or when a facilitator is needed. External consultants should be aware of what the staff has accomplished to this point and should design their programs around the unique needs of this learning community. Consultants should build on the work already done in the school and respect the expertise within the staff.

Steps for Designing Staff Development

Steps for designing staff development in the learning community, summarized from the literature and our own professional experiences, are suggested below.

Relate to the Vision

Shared vision is an important characteristic of the professional learning community (Barth, 1990; Hord, 1997). Professional development should be linked to the vision of the learning community. If the school's vision and goals have not already been collaboratively established, this could be part of the initial professional development activities. See Chapter 2 for details on establishing the vision in a learning community.

Commit to Student Achievement

A commitment to student learning is an integral part of the learning community (Louis & Kruse, 1995). The bottom line for effective professional development is improved student outcomes (NSDC, 2001). In order to determine outcomes, you need to know where your students are. Therefore, you need to collect and analyze data about student work and then determine the student outcomes you want.

Decide on the Areas of Focus

There will probably be many areas that need improvement. Working collaboratively, the staff should determine its priorities for student outcomes.

Identify the Competencies Needed by the Staff

Once the priorities have been determined, consider what knowledge and skills the staff needs to develop in relation to them (Sparks & Hirsh, 1997). Do they need to address improvement in a particular area of math? Are more hands-on strategies needed for science? Are more effective strategies for teaching reading indicated? The staff should be actively involved in this process, as one of the characteristics of professional development in the learning community is increased staff responsibility in planning its professional growth.

Develop a Plan for Professional Development

Using all of the information gathered in the previous steps, work collaboratively to plan professional development. Set objectives for professional development based in large part on student outcomes, as professional development in the learning community is results driven. The plan for professional development should include the evaluation design (Guskey, 2000) and be in accord with the standards for effective professional development (NSDC, 2001).

CONCLUSION

Professional development in a learning community is inextricably entwined with the job of teaching. The characteristics of an effective professional development program are linked to the characteristics of the learning community. The primary focus of an effective professional development program is improved student outcomes. It is results driven and based on curriculum and standards. The process is collaborative, reflective, and ongoing. It takes into account how adults learn and adheres to the standards for staff development. Teachers take increased responsibility for their own professional growth and are active in planning, leading, and evaluating professional development activities. A dynamic and ongoing professional development program is absolutely vital for maintaining the "learning" in a learning community.

ACTIVITIES

1. Design your personal professional development plan using the guidelines suggested in this chapter.

2. With colleagues, identify the greatest professional development needs in your school.

3. Working in collaboration with colleagues, design a staff development program for your learning community to meet these needs.

4. With colleagues, work out an evaluation plan for the staff development program using multiple levels of data.

NOTES

1. "Friday Forum" (Hudson, 2002) summarized with permission from ASCD. All rights reserved.

2. "Designing Professional Development That Works" (Birman et al., 2000) summarized with permission from ASCD. All rights reserved.

4 Learning Through Teamwork

PREVIEW OF THE CHAPTER

In a professional learning community, people work collaboratively to accomplish their collective goals; therefore, teamwork is absolutely essential. Effective teamwork is enhanced by knowledge of group process and dynamics. This chapter will explore aspects of working in groups in learning communities. It will address the following questions:

- How can we overcome barriers to effective teamwork?
- What behaviors promote effective teamwork?
- What are the stages of group development?
- How may conflict among team members be effectively managed?
- What are effective ways for teams to make decisions?
- How should meetings be conducted to promote team development in learning communities?

HOW CAN WE OVERCOME BARRIERS TO EFFECTIVE TEAMWORK?

Harvey Goldstein, the new principal of the Menlo Middle School, would like to transform his school into a learning community. He wants to engage the staff in more teamwork to develop the vision and mission for the school. He would like them to work in groups as they set goals, design activities, look at curriculum, examine student data, and make plans for action. The assistant principal, Mr. Kim, cautions him that the faculty in this school is not used to working in teams. He says most of the teachers prefer to work alone unless they absolutely have to work in groups. He goes on to say that when they do get together in committees, the project bogs down in the bickering that ensues. Mr. Goldstein realizes that a lot of work will have to be done to build the team skills of the staff, but he wants to achieve his vision for the school. What concepts and skills have to be addressed in order to help the staff toward greater productivity and harmony in teamwork?

Mr. Goldstein is right in focusing on team skills in his quest for school improvement. Since much of the work of the professional learning community is carried out in groups, effective teamwork is the community's life's blood. Study groups, learning circles, peer coaching, mentoring, team teaching, and similar approaches all involve teachers learning and working collaboratively. These groups meet both the needs of individual members and of the learning community as a whole. Furthermore, there is an increase in the number of decisions that are made jointly by teams and principals. Teams of teachers share in making decisions on various issues, such as curriculum revision and professional development as well as administrative matters. Teachers of today, who increasingly work in such collaborative situations, need to be knowledgeable of group processes.

Teamwork in the learning community has many benefits, including collaborative learning and shared responsibility for tasks. The synergy created by the group's collective time, energy, and expertise increases productivity. Teams provide enjoyment and a social aspect that enhances work and they are more fun (Katzenbach & Smith, 1993).

Because teamwork is so vital to the learning community, it is important to identify and overcome hindrances to team productivity. Among these barriers are insufficient time for teamwork, inattention to issues of diversity and equity, lack of trust, confusion about goals, inadequacy of administrative support, too large a team, poor communication among group members, insufficient team skills, and inappropriate setting (Plunkett, 1996; Robbins & Finley 1995). Mr. Goldstein has to overcome several of these hindrances as he seeks to transform his school. In preparation, he should read literature on team skills, for example Hackman (1990), Glacel and Robert (1994), and other works mentioned in this chapter. Some suggestions for surmounting these obstacles gleaned from the literature and our own experiences are offered below.

Provide Enough Time for the Group Process

Inadequate time allowance is a big barrier to teamwork in learning communities, as time is very limited in most schools. The fact is that the

Tips for Leaders 4.1

Wine, Cheese, and the Group Process

Like good wine and good cheese, effective group process takes time. Recognize that the group process takes longer than individual action. Allow enough time for the process to go through all its phases. Encourage creative thinking to come up with solutions to the problem of "not enough time," which many learning communities face. If you are in charge of scheduling, try to arrange concurrent planning times for team members.

group process takes longer. If teachers are going to work collaboratively, then time has to be built into the school day to accommodate dialogue, research, and interaction. Many schools have done this successfully, as described in Chapter 3.

Sometimes, enthusiastic teachers banding together can get this time carved out for themselves. For example, in a school where one of the authors was principal, we encouraged increased collaboration. The teachers were very responsive. Since it was a single-grade school, they wanted everyone in the school to have the same preparation time so that they could plan together. The teachers wanted the preparation time at the end of the day since their students went home earlier than the rest of the district. However, the union contract forbade having a preparation period after students went home; it had to be during the children's school day. The teachers banded together, went to their union, and had that clause changed just for them that year. The adjustment worked so well that they continued in that manner for many years, allowing for school-wide collaboration to a degree never previously achieved.

Interestingly enough, the author who was the principal had thought of that solution, but did not suggest it because she knew the teachers would see it as a breech of contract. However, when the teachers collaboratively examined other possibilities and came up with a solution themselves, they all felt they had been a part of the process. This resulted in a feeling of ownership strong enough that they would go to the union to get an exemption to the contract.

Pay Attention to Issues of Equity and Diversity

Paying attention to issues of equity and diversity contributes to a team's success in several ways. Teams are not as effective if they lack the many perspectives on an issue that diversity brings. Diverse teams benefit from the wider range of experiences and viewpoints of its members, which results in more ideas and better decisions (Johnson & Johnson, 2000).

When forming teams in the learning community, it is important to ensure that they are as diverse as possible so that all voices may be heard. This is especially true when learning communities look at their policies and instructional practices and examine curriculum and content. The learning community as a whole and the students suffer if equity and diversity are ignored in these areas. Attention must be given to include ethnic and racial minorities, men and women, and handicapped people on teams whenever possible. It is also good to have a balance of experienced and new teachers. On schoolwide teams, different grade levels and disciplines should be represented. As a principal, one of the authors made it a point to create diverse instructional teams when pairing assistants and teachers and when assigning staff to grade levels so that the children would see and benefit from the range of perspectives thus offered. Achieving diversity in teams may involve additional challenges, but it is worth the effort in order to provide the highest quality education to all of our students, especially with our changing demographics.

Clarify Goals and Objectives

Sometimes, a team fails because the members cannot agree on the purpose or because they may be at odds with one another on specific goals and objectives. In some instances, the charge to the team is unclear. Clarification is important, because shared goals are essential for the team's efforts (Johnson & Johnson, 2000). One of the authors recalls serving on a language arts committee. Some of the members thought that the purpose of the committee was to assess the existing language arts programs. Others argued that the purpose was to develop a new language arts curriculum. The first meeting of the group was really time wasted for all, because the charge was so muddled. Mr. Goldstein, from Menlo Middle School, should ensure that he clearly states his charge to all groups and that members fully understand the purposes of the teams to which they belong.

Provide Strong Administrative Support

Sometimes, teamwork in schools languishes because of lack of administrative support. For teamwork to succeed in schools, it must be nurtured by the administration at both the school level and the district level. Recognition of the teams' work is one form of support. Formally and

Tips for Leaders 4.2

Clear It Up

Frequently a school group falters because the task or the goals become hazy. It is important to stop work on the project and clear up all misunderstandings.

- Query all members regarding their views and concerns about why they are there, what they are trying to accomplish, and how they are going to do it.
- If they are uncertain about the mission, have them review the mission statement.
- If there is confusion about the charge to the team, have the person who gave the charge provide clarification.
- If the group determined its own task and is now in doubt, repeat the process of establishing goals and update the strategies for reaching objectives.

publicly charging the teams with their responsibilities validates the team process in the eyes of the whole community. Celebration of group accomplishments also energizes teamwork. Chapter 9 provides some ways of celebrating team accomplishment. More practical forms of support are needed as well. These include providing resources, supplies, meeting rooms, and time to meet. As a principal who encouraged collaboration among the teachers, one of the authors frequently covered classes herself so that teachers could meet during the day. This practice offers the principal a side benefit of keeping in touch with joys and challenges of teaching. It also helps in maintaining close contact with students. Mr. Goldstein should think carefully about the types of administrative support his groups will need and how he will provide it for them.

Create the Right Sized Team

For teams, bigger is not better; too large a team creates inefficiency (Robbins & Finley, 1995). Teams may be any size depending on the task, but a smaller team is usually more proficient. In most schools, between five and nine members is a manageable size. The smaller team allows for greater participation of individual members and makes scheduling meetings easier. Members also feel a greater responsibility when the team is smaller. Larger groups can be divided into smaller ones. For example, a mathematics curriculum development committee might be broken into grade-level groups but also meet as a whole to assure proper scope and sequence.

Maintain Good Communication

Lack of clear communication among group members or between leaders and groups contributes to failure. Some instances of poor communication that we have observed in schools include insufficient notice of meeting time, agendas not being distributed ahead of time so that members may prepare for the meeting, and members not listening to one another. Allowing enough time for discussion, checking for understanding before ending meetings, and sending meeting minutes and announcements in a timely manner are actions that leaders may take to improve communication within the group. Members may promote good communication by listening to one another respectfully, asking clarifying questions, and expressing their own views clearly. Johnson and Johnson (2000) offer many activities for enhancing communication.

Build Trust

It is very important for the team's productivity that members trust one another (Deutsch, 1973). Even though people may teach in the same building, if they have not worked together on a team they might not know one another well enough for there to be trust between them. Exercises such as "People Search," which both of the authors have used in a wide variety of group situations, can help start the process. "People Search" participants are given a written list of characteristics and they have to go around the room and find people to match as many of them as possible. As part of this activity, participants should be encouraged to have a short conversation with one another. This begins to establish relationships based on common interests. This exercise is recommended as just the first of a series of trust-building activities. Many more advanced trust-building exercises are available in the literature (Harrington-Mackin, 1994). Other strategies for building trust may be found in Chapter 2 of this book.

Provide the Right Setting

Finding the right place to hold team meetings can often be a problem in schools. However, it is very important to find a setting where a team can meet without interruption for the duration of a meeting. Furthermore, members should be able to sit on adult-sized furniture. If there is no room in the school during the day, a municipal library or nearby community center might have a room that the school could use free of charge for meetings. For very important meetings, some districts rent space in a conference center or hotel. One principal of a highly successful urban high school takes her staff to a retreat center once a year.

A word of caution: If using a place outside of the school, be sure that someone physically goes to check out the room. One of the authors still remembers an occasion that occurred many years ago when all of the administrators had to meet to work in groups on a special project. It was decided to book a meeting room at a hotel in a nearby town to avoid distractions in the school buildings. They went expecting a conference room with chairs and tables suitable for a group of 35 people. Instead, they found that the "meeting room" was just a large bedroom with a couple of beds hardly big enough for the group to get into, much less sit down for group work.

Provide Training in Team Skills

People sometimes view team-building activities as a waste of time, but such activities are important for getting acquainted, building trust, clarifying goals, and understanding appropriate group behavior in a professional learning community. Members of teams should be trained to reflect on their group processes and to evaluate the outcomes of their meetings. Team members should discuss what they can do both individually and as a group to make their team more effective and productive. Tools such as those found in Schmuck and Runkel (1994) may be helpful. Administrators as well as teachers should receive training in team-building skills, as principals and supervisors need strong understanding of the group process if they are to lead their staff in collaborative approaches. Mr. Goldstein, the principal of the Menlo Middle School, would be wise to set aside time for training in group process skills for his faculty and to take some training himself.

WHAT BEHAVIORS PROMOTE EFFECTIVE TEAMWORK?

Mr. Goldstein decides to sit in on a grade-level meeting in his school to observe for himself what goes on. When the team leader calls the meeting to order, two teachers go on with their conversation. They continue to make remarks to one another throughout the meeting. The topic of the team meeting is selection of a new text. As the discussion gets started, one teacher raises a question about a conflict in the daily schedule. She dominates the meeting with her complaints, barely giving others a chance to talk. The discussion then digresses. Two teachers get into a heated argument about the schedule, launching personal verbal attacks at each other. When the team leader finally calms things down and gets the discussion back on topic, it is almost time for the meeting to end. Very little has been accomplished. Mr. Goldstein leaves the meeting feeling upset. He feels more enlightened about what Mr. Kim was explaining to him. He feels challenged and even more determined to get the staff functioning productively in teams.

Appropriate Group Behavior

Obviously, the behavior of the teachers in the group Mr. Goldstein observed was neither appropriate nor productive. The literature describes two basic behavior patterns in groups: group- and self-oriented behavior (Plunkett, 1996; Schmuck & Runkel, 1994). Group-oriented behaviors, which include both task- and maintenance-oriented behaviors, expedite the team's progress. Self-oriented behaviors satisfy the individual's emotional and social needs. These terms are discussed further below.

Task-oriented behaviors focus on accomplishing the group's goals. They include such activities as defining the objectives; seeking and giving information; determining strategies; researching, summarizing, and drawing conclusions; and coordinating and scheduling tasks.

Maintenance-oriented activities help to maintain good relationships among group members. Examples of these behaviors include being responsive to others' views, respecting one another's diversity, giving others a chance to participate and communicate, sensing the mood of the group, and designing positive ways of interacting within the group.

Self-oriented behaviors aim toward satisfying the individual's emotional and social needs. Behaviors such as digressing, criticizing, domineering, withdrawing, engaging in personal attacks on others, and indulging in excessive joking are negative examples of this type of behavior. The staff members that Mr. Goldstein observed engaged in excessively negative self-oriented behavior. As a result, they were completely unproductive as a team.

When self-serving behaviors outweigh group-serving behaviors, the group's productivity suffers (Plunkett, 1995). Such behavior impedes the development of collegiality among the members of the learning community. An example of this occurred at a high school faculty meeting where teachers were discussing ways of grading students in an effort to achieve more uniformity. One teacher pleaded for some leniency and consideration of extenuating circumstances when giving students grades. A colleague

---

Tips for Leaders 4.3

Focus the Energy

Members' hidden agendas and emotional issues may cause self-oriented behaviors that hinder the group's progress. Try to find out what they are and focus the group energy back on the task.

---

remarked sarcastically, "You are such a bleeding heart! Why don't we all let the students stay home and not bother to come to class and we'll just mail them all A's." The first teacher took offense and an argument ensued. The result was that the group's attention was diverted from the project at hand, and everyone left the meeting feeling upset and dissatisfied with the lack of progress.

Characteristics of Effective Teams

Effective teams have the expertise necessary for the project and use strategies that are suitable to the task. They are energetic and exert enough effort to complete the task at an acceptable level. The size of the group is small enough to be productive. Team members have mutual goals and share both responsibility and accountability for failure or success.

Members of effective teams exhibit specific behaviors, as pointed out by Katzenbach and Smith (1993), Robbins and Finley (1995), and others. They communicate well, listen to one another, and contribute ideas freely. They can accept criticism and handle conflict effectively. They reach most decisions by consensus and shift leadership among themselves depending on the circumstances and the expertise required. They are committed to the group's objectives, are interested in one another, and celebrate achievements. Mr. Goldstein will have to provide a lot of training and use many strategies to change his staff members into effective teams.

WHAT ARE THE STAGES OF GROUP DEVELOPMENT?

Groups go through a sequence of changes as they mature. It is helpful for leaders and participants to be aware of this and to know what the stages are.

Information Online 4.1

In the forming stage, if the group members do not know each other well, icebreakers will help to dissolve initial awkwardness and make them feel more comfortable. There are several sites on the Internet for such activities. Among them are http://www.topten.org/content/tt.AU20htm and http://www.wholeperson.com/wpa/tr/ice/toc.htm.

This way, they are not unduly discouraged by the fluctuations that occur as part of the natural process. One widely accepted theory, the Tuckman (1965) model, outlines the stages of group development as forming, storming, norming, and performing. Adjourning is often added as an additional stage. Tuckman's stages are presented below, along with strategies for learning communities culled from the literature (Hirsh, 1996, and Robbins & Finley, 1995) and our own knowledge base.

Forming

In the forming stage, individuals transform into a group. Members meet one another, and some may be concerned about being accepted by the group. They learn more about the project, and although they may be optimistic about it, they may also be anxious about the work involved and concerned about the outcomes. Because this is a period of adjustment, there is usually little accomplished on the project itself. Changes in the team later on, such as getting new members, can cause a group that is in a more advanced stage to revert to the forming stage.

Forming Strategies

- Engage in orientation activities at the beginning of this stage.
- Use icebreakers and other exercises to help members get to know one another.
- Initiate trust building activities.
- Clarify the task. If the task has been assigned by someone outside of the group such as a school administrator, have them come and give the charge to the team.
- Decide how the task will be accomplished.
- Explore formal and informal procedures for operating.

Tips for Leaders 4.4

Stand the Storm

Leaders should not try to rush the group through the storming phase. It is important for the group to work through its issues so they don't crop up later. The leader should guide the group through the conflict and not allow it to become destructive.

- Determine group maintenance roles, such as chair and recorder.
- Begin setting norms for behavior and ways of dealing with group problems.
- If feasible and applicable to the project, tour each other's classrooms. It is another way for people to get to know each other professionally and it is a wonderful way to share ideas. The authors have used this technique frequently and have found it very effective.

Storming

As the group continues to meet, it moves into the storming stage. This is the most difficult of all the stages, as it is marked by turmoil. Members complain, argue with each other, and may form factions. The task may seem more difficult than members originally anticipated. Frustration is high and enthusiasm is low in this stage. Very little work is accomplished because so much time and energy are diverted to the strife. It appears from what Assistant Principal Kim said that the groups in Mr. Goldstein's school seldom got past this stage. Some of the following strategies might keep them moving forward.

Storming Strategies

- Present training in conflict resolution.
- Allow the team to work things out, but do not tolerate personal attacks.
- Allow ample discussion time so that all views may be aired.
- Hold a retreat to focus on the group's concerns.
- Review the standards of behavior for group members.
- Use coaching techniques and lots of encouragement to get them through this stage.

Norming

If the group survives storming (and some don't), it moves on to norming, a stage of reduced conflict and greater congeniality. Members now have a sense of team cohesion and more optimism about the outcome of the project. They develop and adhere to rules for team behavior. They also spend much more time on the task and are more productive.

Norming Strategies

- Update group rules for behavior.
- Provide additional training on group process and meeting efficiency.
- Select procedures for decision making.
- Design and implement the action plan.
- Decide on evaluation processes.
- Assign responsibilities relative to the project.
- Establish benchmarks and plan for celebrations.

Performing

Performing is the most productive stage of all. The group has become a proficient working unit and team spirit is at its highest. Team members accept each other and appreciate one another's diversity. They understand their roles, the group expectations, and the task. They are able to implement plans, solve problems, and handle disagreements effectively. Commitment, enthusiasm, and optimism reign. They are on a roll!

Performing Strategies

- Maintain the team spirit.
- Make sure that the group keeps learning.
- Rotate leadership and task responsibilities.
- Use problem-solving, decision-making, and data collection tools.
- Employ strategies for efficient time management.

Adjourning

The final stage, adjourning, brings an end to the project and perhaps to the group. This is a period for closure, reflection, evaluation, and celebration. Members sometimes experience separation anxiety as they approach the finalization of the task and the impending break-up of the group. There is a sense of pride and accomplishment mixed with the sadness of saying good-bye. Individuals often exchange telephone numbers and e-mail addresses and make plans to get together. Sometimes, bonds formed among team members last for many years after the team disbands.

Adjourning Strategies

- Know when to end. Do not continue unnecessarily.
- Assess the processes the group used.
- Evaluate the group's accomplishment.
- Make recommendations for future projects.
- Prepare and package the project presentation, if this is one of the tasks.
- Deliver the final presentation or report.
- Celebrate.

HOW MAY CONFLICT AMONG TEAM MEMBERS BE EFFECTIVELY MANAGED?

You cannot engage in group activities without encountering conflict; conflict is a part of life. This is as true in the learning community as it is in any other organization. Conflict is not necessarily a bad thing. The best decisions are often made as a result of positive conflict. Although conflict is usually more prevalent in the storming stage, it may emerge at any point in the group process. As Deutsch (1973) points out, conflict can be either destructive or constructive, depending on how it is handled: Cooperative approaches to conflict encourage productive outcomes. Mr. Goldstein's staff members did not use conflict in a positive way in the meeting he observed. In order for his faculty to use conflict more productively, they need to learn more about cooperative approaches.

Tips for Conflict Management

The following advice is culled from such experts as Bolman and Deal (1991), Pruitt and Rubin (1986), Fisher and Ury (1981), and Fisher and Brown (1988), and from the experiences of the authors working in schools over the years.

- Seek agreement on basic issues of task and procedure.
- Build rapport through greetings, protocol, and rituals. An example of this is what goes on at negotiations. It absolutely amazed one of the authors the first time she sat in on union negotiations to see the opposing parties engage in friendly small talk and backslapping at

the beginning of each meeting. This happened each time, even though a few minutes later they were in fierce battle with one another.

- Search for common interests, values, and perspectives. Emphasize those things you can agree on.
- Separate the people from the issues. Attack the problem, not the people.
- Rephrase the issue to determine how you can meet the need of both parties.
- Generate many ideas for possible solutions before making a final decision on what to do.
- Base the final decision on an objective standard. It is best to set the criteria ahead of time.

In general, try to build positive relationships by maintaining good communication, being reasonable, and developing mutual acceptance. This is good advice for Mr. Goldstein's faculty as they try to engage more productively in group work.

WHAT ARE EFFECTIVE WAYS FOR TEAMS TO MAKE DECISIONS?

Although groups are formed for many purposes, eventually most have to make decisions. Decisions made by groups are generally more effective than those made by individuals (Harrington-Mackin, 1994; Katzenbach & Smith, 1993). However, making decisions is far more complex for groups than for individuals and takes more time. Engagement in the process is important for group members, because it helps them feel that their input has been respected. They are then more likely to support group decisions. This section will discuss using data to make decisions, offer approaches to group decision making, and give an example of group decision making operating in one school.

Using Data

It is very important to make decisions based on actual data, not just assumptions and subjective perceptions. You need to have data so you can see where you are, set goals, and measure your progress. Data may be test scores, facts, figures, records, reports, and other documents. Data about students are particularly important to the learning community. Offered below are some suggestions for data collection and use compiled from our own knowledge base and sources such as Bonstigl (2001), Holcomb (1999), and Schmoker (2001).

- Know the purpose for collecting data. Be clear on your goals for collecting data and how the data will help improve your learning community. For example, in the Evergreen School discussed in Chapter 1, their Website talks about data-driven instruction to ensure that students meet or exceed the standards.

- Decide what data you will collect. It is often helpful to use disaggregated data about race, gender, socioeconomic class, and so forth, in order to study the subgroups in comparison to the whole group. Collect data from many sources on specific issues, but do not waste time or become overwhelmed with useless data.

- Develop a plan for collecting data and decide what instruments or procedures you will use. The plan should include when and how often the data will be collected and who will collect it.

- Collect your data in an efficient manner. Be sure that the measures, procedures, and method of recording are consistent among all the data collectors. The people collecting the data should be trained in the procedures.

- Get the data into the practitioners' hands. All too often, data are held in the principal's office. Teachers need to see the data and be collaboratively involved in analyzing them. For example, in some schools, teachers examine the test scores in grade-level or subject teams. They manually rank the subtests from the weakest to the strongest to become really familiar with them.

- Use the data as the basis for solving problems and making decisions. Analyze the data and respect the facts shown by them. Take action accordingly. Bonstigl (2001) describes many tools that are helpful to educators for data-driven decision making.

Approaches to Decision Making

In learning communities, teams of teachers take on the responsibility of making many decisions. The literature discusses many methods for group decision making. See, for example, Harrington-Mackin (1994), Plunkett (1996), and Schmuck and Runkel (1994). As there are so many approaches for decision making, groups should select the one most appropriate for a given situation. For example, three approaches frequently used in learning communities are *consensus, majority vote,* and *authority,* each of which works best in certain circumstances, as discussed below.

When the issue is very important to the learning community and commitment from all members is necessary—as, for example when the school is developing its mission statement and working on goals—consensus is the decision-making approach of choice. There must also be sufficient time available for the process of consensus building.

Consensus is reaching a decision that best reflects the combined thinking of all the group members (Johnson & Johnson, 2000). In order to have consensus, everyone must agree with the decision. However, consensus does not mean that every team member is totally satisfied; it means that they support and can live with the decision. Consensus functions most effectively when group members are well informed about the issues and can handle disagreements well. There must be appreciable time for discussion. When checking for consensus, it is important to find out how each individual feels (Harrington-Mackin, 1994). All members, even the ones who are very quiet, should be encouraged to express their views before making the final decision. If everyone does not agree, the discussion needs to continue, because disagreement often stimulates better decisions. However, consensus is not the only way to make decisions in the learning community, nor is it appropriate for every situation.

Majority vote is useful when time is limited or when the issue is not important enough to go through the whole process of consensus building. It is used when deep commitment from each group member is not necessary or when there is a desire to avoid possible conflict. For example, when the faculty is deciding which morning to hold the moving up exercises, they might have a discussion and then take a vote with the majority prevailing.

Authority works best in situations where the decision has to be made quickly, when long-term commitment from the whole group is not required, or when only one person or a few people have the expertise to make the decision. For example, when a pipe bursts in a school lavatory, the principal, with input from the custodian, decides how serious it is and whether to evacuate the building or just a few rooms. She does not call in a team to vote on it or try to build consensus. It is important not to rely on only one approach for making all decisions in the learning community, but rather to select the most appropriate one for each situation.

An Example of Group Decision Making

As a principal, one of the authors advocated shared decision making and collaborative leadership. This was at a central kindergarten school to which all youngsters throughout the town came. The staff and principal worked collaboratively to examine the whole process of students entering school and being assigned to classes. One of the concerns was to create diverse, balanced classes across the school so that all children would have a good learning environment. We wanted classes to be balanced by gender, race, ethnicity, birth date, performance level, and behavior to the greatest extent possible. Other goals were to offer a program that would inform parents about the school and would provide the children with a joyful orientation experience.

The process involved using all of the skills discussed above. Team members did research and collected data. They looked at procedures for entry in other systems. The faculty and staff broke up into smaller teams to handle these various tasks. Both teachers and aides worked on the teams, adding more diversity. After the various committees reported back, the whole group brainstormed and came up with several creative ideas for a new entry and orientation program for the new pupils and their parents.

The resulting orientation program was multilayered and involved the teachers in closely observing children's behaviors. In the process of decision making, consensus building, and program planning, teachers engaged in meaningful conversations about children's behavior and how children learn. These conversations continued after the orientation program and into the school year. The teachers designed forms for observing the new students and discussed appropriate orientation activities. They got consensus on the important decisions, but were satisfied with a majority vote on the minor ones.

In evaluating the process and the results later in the year, parents reported that they liked the new orientation process and that their children had enjoyed themselves. The staff found that they had achieved more of a balance in their classes, thus creating equitable learning environments for all children in the school. An outgrowth of this experience was that the next year, teams of teachers, rather than the principal alone, did the pupil placement. However, the most important outcomes were the sense of ownership the teachers had in the decision-making process and the conversations about teaching and learning that began around this experience and continued into the next school year. This example of group decision making embodies characteristics of the learning community, such as teacher collaboration, shared leadership, and a focus on improving the learning environment for students.

HOW SHOULD MEETINGS BE CONDUCTED TO PROMOTE TEAM DEVELOPMENT IN LEARNING COMMUNITIES?

You probably have been in faculty meetings that seemed interminable, repetitive, and unproductive or in team meetings where one or two members dominated the discussion. Meetings are very important in a learning community, because this is where much of the learning and decision making occurs. The way meetings are conducted can make a big difference in the productivity of the community. Following are some tips for conducting effective meetings.

When a group meets for the first time, special efforts should be made to ensure that the group gets off to a good start. Even though staff members may know each other in a cursory way, they may not be aware of one another's perspectives, backgrounds, working styles or educational philosophies.

Furthermore, the staff may be culturally diverse, and this may have an impact on how they interact as members of a group. Thus it is very important to devote some time to getting to know one another and to building a sense of community. The process is vital and should not be hurried through. It is also important in initial meetings to set the ground rules and establish norms for group behavior. Glacel and Robert (1994), Plunkett (1996), and Schmuck and Runkel (1994) suggest specific steps that should be taken before, during, and after meetings for greatest effectiveness. Some of their ideas as well as some that we have learned from many years of running meetings are incorporated in the suggestions below.

Before Meetings

Planning for meetings is essential for success. First, decide whether the meeting is necessary or whether the matters can be taken care of through e-mail or some other means. If a meeting is the best approach, decide who should attend, reserve the space, and make sure that it is available for the entire length of the meeting. Plan the agenda and distribute it, along with any information or data people need to prepare for the meeting, in a timely manner. On the day of the meeting, arrive early to assure that the equipment is in working order and the room is prepared for the meeting.

During Meetings

There are several procedures to observe during meetings to attain the greatest productivity. Begin on time, follow the agenda, and keep the group on task. Encourage participation of all members and keep order. Periodically, it is good to check on the group process. Have some members focus on how well the group is accomplishing its task and report to the rest of the group. Tools such as those found in Glacel and Robert (1994) are helpful in this task. Before the meeting is over, summarize and make sure that each member knows what is expected for the next meeting.

After Meetings

After meetings, relay information, usually in the form of minutes, to those who need to know, but maintain confidentiality regarding sensitive meeting discussions. Check that assignments are understood and carried out. Assess the effectiveness of the session and plan accordingly for the next meeting.

CONCLUSION

Is teamwork important to learning communities? The response from the literature and our experience is a definite "Yes!" Working in teams is the essence of learning communities. As Joyce and Showers (1988) point out, faculties that are organized into study teams and that work together for the improvement of the school are more cohesive, have higher morale, and are more responsive to initiatives from one another and from administrative leadership. In our roles as school administrators and trainers of school leaders, we have found that the team process promotes a greater spirit of community and a more positive focus of energies toward improvement of the school. Better solutions result through group problem solving and decision making because of the diverse perspectives the members bring. Furthermore, there is greater support for decisions in which all have had the opportunity for input. Teamwork brings great strength and vitality, and is a vital element of the learning community.

ACTIVITIES

1. Think of the groups in your learning community. What are their purposes? Which ones are formal and which informal? Which are temporary and which permanent? How was the leadership identified for the groups?

2. Observing what happens in groups improves our understanding of group dynamics and enhances our effectiveness in the group. Study the behaviors of members in your group. Which ones are task- and maintenance-oriented? Which are self-oriented? Is there a healthy balance? How is the behavior of the group members affecting the productivity of the team?

3. *The staff development committee at Menlo Middle School had been meeting for about three weeks and everything was going well. However, at the fourth meeting, things appeared to be falling apart. Squabbling broke out among the members to the point where they could not get through the agenda. The next meeting was just as bad. The principal heard about this and is considering dissolving the committee. He thinks it is taking too much time and that the arguing in the group meetings may spread conflict throughout the school.* What is happening here? What advice would you give the principal and the teachers?

4. *Mr. Patel is setting up initial meetings to revise the third-grade curriculum. Some of the teachers are new to the grade and one is new to the school.* What should Mr. Patel consider as he plans these meetings? What activities should be included in the first two meetings? Help him plan the first two meetings.

5 Learning Through Study Groups

PREVIEW OF THE CHAPTER

Across the country, school reformers have recognized that conversations among administrators, supervisors, and teachers are a critical aspect of building the professional community needed for successful school restructuring. Finding ways to create an environment in which all participants can share and increase their knowledge, exchange ideas, create new professional relationships, and reinforce existing ones is one of the ongoing challenges faced by those who want to create a community of learners. In discussing professional community as a critical aspect of school improvement, Louis et al. (1996) state,

> While individual professionalism is desirable, active work in a professional group is also important to increasing teachers' sense of craft and their overall commitment to work contexts that are increasingly difficult and demanding. (p. 758)

Traditionally, conversations among educators have taken place in such forms as school-based management teams, cabinet meetings, and grade-level or subject-specific meetings. In the current literature, however, the use of study groups is being discussed as a professional development strategy with the potential for helping to build communities of professional practice (Birchak et al., 1998; Lewis, 1997). Accordingly, the following questions will be addressed in this chapter:

- What is a study group?
- What are the purposes and benefits of study groups for a community of learners?

- How do you initiate a study group?
- How can teacher book study groups be planned and conducted?

WHAT IS A STUDY GROUP?

Elementary School #1 in the Menlo School District has a population of more than 400 students, approximately 45 of whom qualify for special education. The student population represents various ethnic and socioeconomic groups. Next year, the school will implement an inclusion program and all special education students will be assigned to regular classes where they will receive mandated services. Special education teachers and/or other support personnel will be assigned to work in the inclusion classrooms to ensure that all children are provided with mandated services.

Many of the teachers are concerned about their readiness to work as part of an instructional team and about their ability to ensure that all the children in the newly structured classes receive appropriate developmental and supplemental instruction. The principal, David Somers, who is making plans for the new educational program, has become aware of the tension among the teachers about the new roles and responsibilities that they will have to assume. The district's director of curriculum, Jack Carson, recommended that the principal invite the teachers to form study groups on inclusion in order to prepare to implement the new inclusion program. Mr. Somers has decided to approach his staff about starting such study groups in the school. What does he need to know about study groups before introducing his idea to the faculty, staff, and parents?

A study group is simply a gathering of people who meet on a regularly scheduled basis to address issues that the group members have agreed to study. By its very nature, a study group organizes a group of teachers into a community of learners. We have worked with study groups that have come together based on similar interests, instructional levels, or curricular areas.

Study groups are recognized as a job-embedded approach to the professional growth of teachers. By initiating study groups, Jack Somers, the principal of Menlo School #1, will provide his teachers with a structured process through which they can collegially learn about and resolve the issues associated with implementing the district's new inclusion program. The learning resulting from their participation in study groups will be embedded in the daily tasks which their carry out as they implement inclusion strategies in their classrooms.

One of our first experiences with study groups occurred in a school in which the authors served as consultants. Three teachers had voluntarily been meeting during their lunch period to share ideas and discuss the problems they were having in implementing a new district-mandated mathematics program. The teachers approached the principal, informed her about how beneficial their meetings had been, and suggested that other teachers who were experiencing difficulty might find the meetings useful. They asked the principal for permission to circulate a memo in which they would invite interested teachers to join their lunchtime discussions. The principal approved their request and offered to provide them with the assistance and support needed to make their efforts successful. Twelve teachers responded that they were interested in participating in the group's discussions.

At the initial meeting of the expanded group of teachers, it was discovered that many issues needed to be resolved before the group could begin conversations about the curriculum. Because the teachers had different lunch hours, the newly formed teacher-initiated, teacher-led group held its first meeting after the school day ended. Several teachers who had expressed interest in the group were unable to attend on the day selected for the meeting; one teacher thought it would be a good idea to hold the meetings before school; other teachers were surprised that the principal had not been asked to attend the meeting; and one teacher felt that, because the group was teacher-initiated, they should meet at a site away from the school.

Not only did the teachers have different ideas about the group's goals and how the goals could be accomplished, but they also had different reasons for attending the meeting. There were several teachers who joined the group because they had a need for in-depth dialogue with their peers about the new curriculum. Two teachers hoped the group would invite guest speakers from a college to meet with the group on a regular basis to discuss the math program, as they did not think that the teachers had the expertise needed to resolve instructional issues. One teacher had attended the meeting as the representative of the teachers' association; another thought they were meeting to modify the curriculum; and one teacher came to the meeting out of curiosity.

The teachers in the scenario described above learned that bringing a group of teachers together to form a discussion group calls for careful planning, good communication, and an in-depth understanding of the issues associated with teacher study groups. Teacher-leaders and administrators who want to successfully organize teacher discussion groups must have a clear understanding of the purpose of the group, how to plan for group

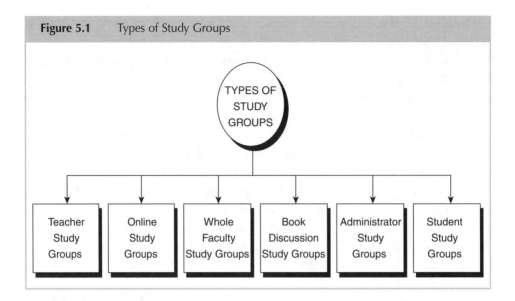

Figure 5.1   Types of Study Groups

meetings, the barriers to implementation, and strategies for initiating and sustaining study groups.

Study groups can therefore be used to provide the framework for the development of a culture of collaboration and the building of community, as they have the same characteristics that are associated with learning communities. The study group strategy positions teachers and administrators at the center of their teaching/learning environment, because they make the decisions about what the group is to study, and while studying, they learn about each other and learn to work together. Within a school or district, different types of study groups can provide the context for building a learning community.

Types of Study Groups

Much has been written about the structure, functions, and activities of study groups (Birchak et al., 1998; Cramer, Hurst, & Wilson, 1996; Murphy & Lick, 2001) as one of the cornerstones for building community in schools. Teacher study groups, administrator study groups, whole-faculty study groups, online study groups, student study groups, and book study groups can all provide schools with part of the infrastructure that promotes collaboration, reflective dialogue, the sharing of personal practice, and teamwork that reinforces commitment to a school's shared vision and values. Each type of study group is briefly discussed below.

Teacher Study Groups

Teacher study groups may take many forms (see Figure 5.1). They may be initiated by teachers or administrators to promote dialogue about professional issues of mutual concern and to advance the teachers' growth and development. These groups will frequently convene at lunchtime in a teacher's classroom or some other site in the school; they may also choose to meet before or after school the school day (Cramer et al. 1996).

Currently, in our work with schools, we have observed that the practice of forming these groups is proliferating. An informal survey that we conducted suggests several reasons that teachers choose to voluntarily give of their time to participate in these group activities. Often, they have a need to engage in professional dialogue that is not being addressed in the school's traditional staff development program. In schools that have a major need for school reform, voluntary participation in study groups is a way of alleviating teachers' strong desire to find meaningful solutions to the persistent problems that impede their students' educational progress and that plague their everyday lives at work. Having little confidence in the path to reform that has already been initiated in their schools, these teachers have set out to identify and study alternative ways of improving their institutions.

Administrators' Study Groups

Principals and supervisors can also benefit greatly from participation in study groups with their peers. Meeting in groups, they can explore their beliefs about effective leadership styles and behaviors, and can reflect on the quality of their practice. Typically, these groups may be organized by the leadership of the school district, by a principals' association, or by a group of concerned principals. Commenting on her work with study groups of principals, Nancy Mohr (1998) states,

> Principals must be leaders of learning in their schools. Principals who want teachers to be in study groups can encourage the process in several ways, but they probably can't teach others how to be learners if they do not acknowledge their own need for on going learning. (p. 43)

When a principal shares information about a program with peers and has a regularly scheduled opportunity to discuss the program's effectiveness and limitations, the entire group gets better at understanding and analyzing problems from a leadership perspective. Take, for example, an urban school district we worked with that was in the process of implementing the New Language Arts performance standards. A group of principals and assistant principals in the district meet on a regular basis to share ideas and experiences, read and discuss related literature, and solve

---

Information Online 5.1

Read the publication *Electronic Collaboration: A Practical Guide for Educators* (Northeast and Islands Regional Educational Laboratory at Brown University, 1999), available at http://www.lab.brown.edu/public/ocsc/ collaboration.guide/keying.into.shtml. In-depth information is provided about the many forms of electronic collaboration, but the focus is on discussion groups, as they are the most common online collaborative activity.

---

problems associated with their attempts to carry out the initiative. By establishing a study group on the new standards, the administrators are meeting their own needs as well as the district's mandate to carry out the innovation. Additionally, the study group will afford them the opportunity to practice many of the communication skills they need when working with teachers, including listening, consensus building, and giving and receiving feedback. These are skills that will serve them well when they interact with teachers (Mohr, 1998).

Online Study Groups

Educators increasingly collaborate electronically in a variety of ways. Collaboration is taking place via the Internet employing such tools as e-mail, video conferencing, and various sites on the World Wide Web to examine and improve instructional practices and to integrate technology into teaching and learning. In online communities, educators participate in study groups, literature discussion groups, chat rooms, displaying and/or developing documents, videoconferencing, and online courses and workshops.

Study groups can use the Web to work, learn together, conduct research, and disseminate and share information. In spite of its escalating popularity, electronic collaboration does have its limitations. The absence of shared surroundings and vocal interaction results in a form of communication that is not as rich as what educators experience in face-to-face meetings.

Whole-Faculty Study Groups

Whole-faculty study groups is a model in which all faculty members in a given school participate in small study groups that focus on schoolwide

Tips for Leaders 5.1

Forming Student Study Groups

Instructional leaders should encourage their teachers to initiate student study groups as one aspect their instructional program. In addition to promoting collaborative learning, increasing students' knowledge of course content, and developing students' leadership skills, these groups are an important aspect of the process by which an entire school is transformed into a learning community. If student study groups are to be successful, teachers must ensure that the students have the skills needed to participate in the process.

improvement in teaching and learning. In this model, which has become widely known through the work of Carlene Murphy (Murphy & Lick, 2001), at least 75% of the teachers in the school must endorse the process before it can be implemented in a school. All teachers in the school convene regularly, in groups of three to six, in a process that is driven by the school's improvement plan. Murphy and Lick (2001) describe the process as "a management process for bringing about major change and learning improvement" (p. 17). The focus is on organizational issues that have an impact on student learning, and it is expected that participation in these groups will result in the implementation of new instructional skills. In whole-faculty study groups, each member in turn takes on the leadership role. This contributes to the building of a learning community by providing a structured process through which every teacher has a planned opportunity to develop his or her leadership skills through a collaborative process (Murphy & Lick, 2001).

Student Study Groups

Study groups for students are often structured by classroom teachers to help students develop and utilize study strategies and to master course content. These groups promote collaboration among students and facilitate the sharing of knowledge and materials. They also provide a support network for students and opportunities for social interaction (Cramer et al., 1996).

> ## Tips for Leaders 5.2
>
> ### Inform Your Teachers About Study Groups
>
> To stimulate interest in a study group, distribute a journal article on such groups to your teachers. To motivate and ascertain their interest in starting a study group,
>
> - Follow up on an informal basis by engaging individual teachers in conversations about the article.
> - Follow up formally by discussing the article in a faculty meeting. Promote shared leadership by asking a teacher to lead the discussion.

Book Study Groups

Book study groups are formed when a group of educators come together to read, discuss, and analyze a series of agreed-upon books in light of their implications for their professional and/or personal lives. A full discussion of how to conduct a book discussion group is provided later in this chapter, in the section How Can Teacher Book Study Groups Be Planned and Conducted?

WHAT ARE THE PURPOSES AND BENEFITS OF STUDY GROUPS FOR A COMMUNITY OF LEARNERS?

Study groups have many purposes. They serve to build professional community in schools. Participating teachers may learn new instructional techniques, research a topic of interest to the group, resolve everyday problems in school, or keep abreast of current educational literature. Such groups may be formed to analyze and study curriculum and student work samples. Teachers in study groups will feel more empowered as they acquire additional knowledge about teaching and learning (Birchak et al., 1998; Murphy & Lick, 2001).

As discussed in the literature, and as we have found in our work, a school derives many benefits from the study group process. Teachers as individuals benefit because they have a structured process from which they can draw encouragement and support and reduce teacher isolation. They also have a planned opportunity to sharpen their group problem-solving, leadership, and communication skills by discussing and sharing their points of view. The school as a whole benefits because study groups can serve to institutionalize district and school site initiatives and to focus school reform efforts on improved student learning (Birchak et al., 1998; Murphy & Lick, 2001).

In some schools, study groups are viewed as a way of sustaining the school's mission, shared vision, and shared values. A case study describing a study group meeting is provided below.

Case Study: A Study Group Meeting

This case describes a meeting of a study group in a sixth through eighth-grade middle school. Fourteen teachers and one staff developer voluntarily participated in the study group, which met after school twice a month for 90 minutes. The teachers had decided that the focus of their study group discussions for the year would be the implementation of the New York City Performance Standards in Literacy. This topic was an issue of major concern for the teachers, as they were required to demonstrate that they were implementing the standards in their daily lessons.

As agreed upon at the last meeting of the group, the staff developer had identified a journal article, which was distributed to the teachers in advance of the meeting. The staff developer, who served as a resource for the group, had helped to identify some of the specific activities to get the group meeting launched. She developed a list of questions and exercises for the meeting, observed the activities, and, where appropriate, modeled some related student tasks described in the standards document. The staff developer attended the meeting, but did not lead it. Each meeting of this group was led by a different teacher who volunteered for the leadership role.

The group was wrestling with the standards for literacy that were being implemented by the New York City public schools. Their focus was on what specific indicators really meant and how to effectively teach them. Their approach was to experience the tasks as students experienced them. Through metacognition, they could then learn to refine their instructional approaches. The teachers completed the task and responded to questions similar to the ones that were required of their students. The questions had been devised by the staff developer who was in attendance at the meeting.

The discussion was lively and even evolved into a debate at one point. Teachers gave their ideas, asked questions of one another, reflected, and really probed all aspects of the exercise and its meaning for their students.

Having carried out an activity that was modeled after a task required of students seemed to bring the teachers to a greater understanding of how to effectively carry out instruction for that standard. They worked cooperatively, sharing thoughts and strategies. They also engaged in an activity designed to deepen their understanding of the standards and then probed how strategies for ongoing assessment could be developed. Other activities during this session focused on samples of student work that were distributed to teachers. They worked in triads to examine ways of matching the student work samples to the rubric to determine the levels of student performance and make suggestions to the student. They encouraged one another to give evidence for their conclusions.

The staff developer and the teachers felt that the biggest obstacle for their group was finding adequate time to perform all the tasks needed to make the meeting successful. Some teachers stated that, initially, they were very uncomfortable about publicly challenging the opinions of other teachers, but that over time they had overcome this fear.

In response to a question on how the study group differed from their regular staff meetings, the staff developer stated that there was much more participation and reflection on the part of the teachers both in the meetings themselves and in classrooms.

Review of their study group logs indicate that the group members tried out the strategies from these sessions in their classrooms and reported on the results at the next meeting. The teachers felt that all members of the group gradually became more comfortable with one another and acquired a deeper understanding of a topic when it was openly discussed and debated at their meetings. They shared their successes and expressed their concerns, complained less about implementing the standards, and were more willing to try new things. Other changes observed were an increased interest in professional literature related to the topics being studied and a heightened interest on the part of participants in attending professional workshops relative to the study topics. The staff developer said that this type of professional behavior did not occur on as regular a basis before the study group was launched.

HOW DO YOU INITIATE A STUDY GROUP?

The experiences of the teachers in the case study make it clear that careful planning must be a part of beginning and sustaining a study group. This section will focus on strategies for the implementation of teacher study groups. The ideas and strategies presented are not to be followed in a step-by-step fashion, but are to be selected and adjusted to meet the particular needs of your teachers and school. The topics covered include (a) the role of the principal, (b) strategies for conducting planning meetings, and (c) strategies for conducting successful study group meetings.

Role of the Principal/Supervisor

The principal and supervisors play an important role in the implementation of study groups. Therefore, they must acquire an in-depth knowledge of how the process works and should develop the process skills needed for guiding the faculty.

Before initiating study groups in a school, the principal should take steps to ensure that the staff sees the value of and is at a readiness level for participation in the study group process. It is important that any approach used to introduce a faculty to study groups or any other innovation be done in a manner that promotes collaborative interaction between and among teachers and supervisors and that is respectful of teachers' role as decision makers. There are several strategies that we recommend to principals who want to make their teachers aware of the benefits of participation in study groups (see Tips for Leaders 5.3).

Once study groups have been initiated in a school, the principal should become their chief supporter (Birchak et al., 1998; Murphy & Lick, 2001). This point cannot be overemphasized. In our experience, study groups do not become a viable professional development strategy without the public support of a school's principal. The principal must take steps to sustain and institutionalize them because of the continuous learning opportunity that they provide for teachers. The strategies provided in Tips for Leaders 5.4 can be used for this purpose.

We have tested these strategies in our work in schools as study group facilitators. Supervisors and teacher-leaders who successfully used the strategies found that teachers seemed more willing to share ideas with one another and to discuss with them what works and does not work. Through the study groups, teachers collaboratively addressed particular issues of instruction and tackled pedagogical problems they faced. Often, the supervisors observed greater staff participation in the study group meetings than in the regular faculty and team meetings.

Principals' Participation in Study Group Meetings

In some schools in which we have worked, we have observed principals who served as active participants in group meetings. This does not, however, necessarily mean that those in formal leadership positions *should* participate in the group meetings. Birchak and her colleagues (Birchak

---

Tips for Leaders 5.3

Strategies for Initiating Teachers' Interest in a Study Group

- Conduct awareness sessions on study groups for your teachers. It may be helpful to have a teacher who has participated in study groups, a district office staff member, or a consultant from a local college with experience in working with study groups conduct the session.
- Encourage members of the teaching staff to visit a Website on the topic of study groups to learn about the value of study groups as a professional development tool. The teachers can share this information with their colleagues at grade-level, content-area, and/or general faculty meetings.
- Arrange for members of the staff to visit study groups in action in neighboring schools and to report back to the faculty about their visits. We have found that this process can be facilitated by curriculum coordinators at the district level who can identify schools that have effective study group initiatives in place.
- Distribute articles to the staff about study groups and informally engage the teachers, individually and in groups, in a discussion of the content of the articles.
- Establish a pilot by inviting a few teachers to form a study group on a topic that is related to your school improvement plan. The teachers can report back to the faculty on the results of their study and will serve as catalysts for starting other study groups in your school.

---

et al., 1998) make several important observations around the issue of principal participation. They note that, when principals or supervisors attend the meetings on a regular basis, their presence tends to restrict the depth and breadth of the discussion. They therefore argue that the principal's participation should be a decision made by the teachers.

We have observed that, because the principal is the person who assumes the role of their evaluator or supervisor, teachers are often reluctant to divulge their opinions fully or discuss content or instructional issues about which they feel less than competent in the supervisor's presence. In some schools, however, we have observed that a principal's

Tips for Leaders 5.4

Strategies for Sustaining Teachers' Interest in Study Groups

- Disseminate information about the work being done by study groups to the entire staff as well as to the district leadership and school community at large (Murphy, 2001). Share information about their work at faculty and team meetings and in school newsletters and bulletins.
- Have an understanding of the staff development needs of your teachers.
- Demonstrate commitment by participating in planning meetings at which you listen to teachers, help to build consensus, and give and receive feedback from the participants.
- Attend training sessions conducted for the study groups in your school and periodically attend a group meeting.
- Provide the group with the necessary resources, including time, to meet and carry out their work. Purchase study materials and relevant books for the study group's activities and professional library (Birchak et al., 1998; Murphy & Lick 2001).
- Sponsor study group attendance at workshops related to the topics under study.
- Validate study groups by publicly recognizing and celebrating their accomplishments (Murphy & Lick 2001).
- As a culminating activity, supervisors might want to plan a seminar/social for all study group participants.

participation can break down barriers and promote a sense of collaboration between the teaching staff and its principal, as their leader learns more about the teachers' beliefs, concerns, and needs. In these schools, the comfort level and existing relationships between the teachers and their leader were respectful and collegial. Whatever role they assume in study group meetings, principals should validate and must support the activities of study groups because such groups provide a collaborative structure that contributes to the building and maintenance of community (Birchak et al., 1998; Murphy & Lick, 2001).

Figure 5.2	Planning Meeting Agenda

INFORMATIONAL/PLANNING
MEETING ON STUDY GROUPS

From: Subschool Lead Teacher

To: Classroom and Supplement Teachers

Subject: All teachers are invited to attend an informational
               meeting on study groups

PROPOSED AGENDA

- What are the purposes and benefits of study groups for our school and faculty?
- Who can join the study group?
- What topic do we need to focus on at our meetings?
- When, where, and at what time will our study group meet?
- What rules and procedures should we use in conducting meetings?
- Who will facilitate the study group meetings?
- Will belonging to a study group mean that participants have more "work" to accomplish?
- Other concerns and questions.

Case Study: Conducting a Planning Meeting

We have noticed that the study group experience is helpful in breaking down barriers between teachers and getting them to talk to one another. For example, one school building in which we worked had been restructured into four subschools. Normally, the faculties from the four subschools did not meet even though their students used the same physical education facilities, lunchroom, and auditorium and were served by the same after-school programs. The use of these facilities and programs by four subschools created several ongoing logistical, instructional, and programming problems. The leaders of the subschools invited interested teachers from all the subschools to a meeting to plan study groups on topics of interest to the teachers. We worked with the leaders to develop an agenda for the planning meeting (Figure 5.2).

Teachers from the different subschools formed several groups and met on a regularly scheduled basis to discuss problems that were common to all groups in the building. The study groups broke barriers that existed across the schools, across the grades, and even across the floors. Now, teachers who normally would not have contact with another were working together to address operational instructional issues they have in common. The support of the principals and supervisors served to validate and embed these groups as a factor in the professional development of the instructional staff.

Strategies for Conducting Planning Meetings

Careful planning is required to ensure the success of a study group. More than one planning meeting may be necessary to establish the parameters within which the group will work. Consistent with learning community characteristics, it is important that decisions be reached by consensus. This provides teachers with a sense of ownership and empowerment regarding the new initiative. Supervisors should be aware that setting a collegial tone during planning meetings will often set the stage for a smooth introduction and acceptance of study groups in their schools.

In the planning process, preliminary agreements must be reached on an array of issues, such as questions about who is to participate, the size of the study group, meeting times and places, group leadership, the content to be studied, and other resources that may be needed (Birchak et al., 1998). The list of questions and answers provided in Tips for Leaders Tips 5.5 can be used to help prepare for planning meetings.

Strategies for Conducting Study Group Meetings

Murphy and Lick (2001) recommend that a study group collectively establish norms for group behavior during the meetings. They advise that meetings should begin and end at the designated time and that routines be established for the closure of each meeting. For example, at the end of each meeting, the group may make decisions about the objective for the next meeting; they may develop a process for evaluating the meeting; and they should complete a brief summary describing what occurred at the meeting. They also advise that copies of the summary be distributed at the next meeting so that each member can review past discussions when necessary, identify connections between past discussions and new ideas, and maintain a sense of continuity with respect to accomplishing individual and group goals. Study group meetings must address the needs of the individual group members as well as the agreed-upon goal of the group (Cramer et al., 1996). To ensure that all needs are addressed, it is important that each participant has an opportunity to contribute to the discussion. The

Tips for Leaders 5.5

Questions to Be Considered When Organizing Study Groups

Who will participate in the study group?

Membership in a group may include teachers from one grade level, content area teachers or specialists, supervisors or administrators, or any group of educators who are interested in and committed to studying a particular topic.

What will be the size of the group?

Ideally, a teacher study group will consist of between 10 and 20 participants (Birchak et al., 1998). This will allow adequate opportunity for all members to participate in group discussions.

Where and how often will the group meet?

A regularly scheduled place and time for group meetings must be identified (Murphy & Lick, 2001). If the group members all come from the same school, they can meet in an available classroom, media center, or other available space in the school. If they come from different schools, they can rotate the meeting site or select a site that is convenient for the members. A group may meet weekly or every two weeks.

When will the study groups meet?

Identifying a regular scheduled time to meet is one of the biggest hurdles faced by study group members. An administrator may be able to develop a modified teaching schedule and regularly schedule a meeting during the school day. In some schools, teachers voluntarily come in before the beginning of the school day, meet at lunchtime, or remain after school for their meetings. At other sites, the principal arranges for a shortened school day or schedules a common preparation period for teachers in the same study

Tips for Leaders 5.5 *(Continued)*

	group. Another option is for the principal to arrange for the group to meet while students are in an assembly (Birchak et al., 1998; Murphy & Lick, 2001).
How will leadership be provided for the group?	A decision must be made about the leadership of the group. Shared or rotating leadership is generally more desirable than having one person assume the leadership role. Rotating leadership is more likely to engender commitment to the work being carried out by the group and to develop the leadership capabilities of all group members (Murphy & Lick, 2001). Expertise in the topic under discussion is not needed to assume the role of group leader. Willingness, the ability to be a facilitator, and having the necessary group process skills are important assets for assuming a leadership role (Birchak, 1998).
What topics will the group study?	A group may select a topic to be the focus of their study from a variety of alternatives. Participants should establish the relationship between the topic being studied and improved student achievement. They may decide to carry out research on a topic of mutual interest to the group, to conduct studies of books or professional literature, to study a district or school initiative, to study specific instructional issues that will improve their teaching or supervisory skills, or to visit a site where a program if interest is being implemented. A popular activity for study groups is the study of a

Tips for Leaders 5.5 *(Continued)*

	professional book or the analysis of articles in educational journals that relate to teaching and learning in their school.
What procedures should the group use?	• Norms for group behavior must be established at the first group meeting (Murphy & Lick, 2001). • Roles and responsibilities—secretary, timekeeper, etc.—must be identified and assigned. • If necessary, formal training or exercises in the processes that contribute to group effectiveness may be needed for the success of the study group.
What materials/ resources are needed?	• Study groups need a place in which to conduct regularly scheduled meetings. • Relevant books and copies of articles from educational journals should be made available. • Budgetary consideration should be given to providing relevant videotapes, subscriptions to professional journals, and software for study group activities. • It is recommended that a brief summary be kept of each meeting recapping the topic, discussions, and outcomes (Murphy & Lick, 2001).

participation of all members must be valued and cultivated. One strategy that a group might consider is taking five minutes at the beginning of the meeting for all participants to share relevant information about their classroom practice as it relates to the topic under discussion (Murphy & Lick, 2001) We use this strategy in working with study groups, because it serves to reinforce the primary purpose of the group—to focus collaboratively on teaching and learning.

Problems can be avoided by assuring that teachers receive journal articles and other reading matter for the month well ahead of the meetings. During the meetings, teachers should be encouraged to share their reactions to the readings and to relate what they have read to their daily teaching activities.

The Use of Technology by Teacher Study Groups

Study groups can be used to enhance teachers' knowledge and comfort level with the use of technology. For many teachers, using the computer means learning something brand-new. As facilitators, we are integrating technology into study group activities to expand teachers' learning experiences not only by allowing them to communicate with one another, but also to encourage them to seek out the experiences of other teachers, to learn about unfamiliar ways of teaching, and to reflect on their own classroom instructional practices. Teachers who use the computer as part of study group activities become more at ease in introducing Web-based learning activities to their students. The building of community is enhanced as group members meet and collaborate face-to-face at group meetings, while at the same time they collectively explore new learning opportunities via the Internet in a nonthreatening environment.

Once a teacher study group is formed and the members have achieved a degree of collegiality, the use of e-mail can be introduced. It is suggested that the members of the group meet in a school computer laboratory and that, if necessary, training be provided that allows the participants to use e-mail to build community in the following ways:

- Chose someone in the group who is comfortable with technology to serve as the group e-mail facilitator. The facilitator will make a master e-mail contact list and send group messages to the study group participants. If this method is chosen, we recommend that all members serve in this role for a period of time to give everyone the opportunity to learn more about and become more comfortable with the use of technology.
- Share the list of e-mail addresses with all group members. They can then communicate with one another by e-mail. Make a list of the e-mail addresses of any teachers in the school who would like to receive information by e-mail about upcoming study group activities.

Members of a study group can build community electronically through a number of activities. Depending on their level of comfort, the study groups with which we have worked have gradually introduced the following activities into their plan of study. They have

- Learned to use the Internet to obtain information about a topic that the group is studying.
- Identified articles on a topic of interest for the entire group to read.
- Discussed the implementation of the teaching practices explored in the study group meetings. This online activity provides opportunities for reflecting on improving learning, the ultimate goal of the learning community. Additionally, it gives study groups that meet on a monthly basis a way to build community between meetings.
- Conducted training sessions in the use of e-mail and the Internet and invited other teachers on the faculty to participate.
- Searched for and found lesson plans for a topic they were planning to introduce to their students. They nurtured community by collaborating on the development of a Website for their school.

The tasks associated with these activities have often served to motivate and sustain a group. Additionally, the study group community is extended across the entire faculty when other teachers in the school receive useful information by e-mail about study group activities. Our own experiences suggest that these activities can foster a spirit of collegiality and teamwork when they are valued and supported by those in leadership positions in the school. Extensive information about electronic collaboration and about some of the ideas and activities discussed in this section can be found at the Website discussed in Information Online 5.1.

HOW CAN TEACHER BOOK STUDY GROUPS BE PLANNED AND CONDUCTED?

In many schools, book study groups are being formed as a vehicle for launching and sustaining collaboration among teachers and staff. We have found that book discussion groups can be successfully used as an avenue for cultivating collaboration and encouraging the personal growth of teachers. This section will describe how to plan for the implementation of book study groups.

Those in leadership positions use the study of a book in many different ways. Superintendents and principals have found book discussion groups to be an effective strategy for ongoing professional development of school leaders. For example,

- In an article in the *School Administrator*, Smit (2001) describes how a district leadership team, led by their superintendent, has been involved in a book discussion group. The process includes (a) reading a professional book selected by the superintendent relevant to an existing issue in their district, (b) meeting to collaboratively review what they have read, (c) reflecting on what they have learned and how it relates to their leadership responsibilities, and (d) renewing their thinking by staying current with the knowledge in the field.

The principal of an urban school undergoing reform (in which one of the authors served as facilitator) reports on his use of a strategy he had read about in the literature. He uses the discussion of a current best seller to initiate and sustain collaboration among the members of his school leadership team. He selects an interesting book that enables the team to discuss and bond around issues that, on the surface, are unrelated to the challenges they face as they struggle to reform a school that has been historically mired in failure. At their meetings, they judge the book before and after the discussion to see if and why the discussion causes any of the team members to change their ideas about the book. The principal finds that his team is able to collectively engage in discussion, reflect on their ideas, and share their points of view. They learn to fashion agreement as they experience the process by which individual group members can change their positions and use discussion to reach consensus. The final activity is the exchange of ideas about the value of the book study. Over time, the process has strengthened the bonds among members of the team. It has provided them with a scheduled opportunity to nurture collegiality and develop the trust needed to carry out their work.

Planning for a Book Study Group

Recently, one of the writers was requested by a group of teachers in an early childhood school to assist in the planning of a teacher book club. As a first step, the facilitator suggested that, in order to solicit the participation of other interested teachers, a memo should be prepared and disseminated to the staff describing the purpose and activities of the proposed book club and inviting interested teachers to participate.

Once the interested teachers had been identified, they were invited to a planning meeting, which was attended by the facilitator and led by a teacher volunteer. At the meeting, the first step taken by the teacher-leader was to encourage the other teachers to share their reasons for wanting to participate in a book discussion group. This was followed by an open discussion and final decisions were made about the dates, place, and time for the group to meet. A teacher volunteered to take brief notes summarizing each meeting held during the current school semester.

The teachers then began to struggle with the issue of group leadership. The facilitator discussed the benefits of having a group discussion leader

| **Figure 5.3** | Representative Discussion Questions for a Teacher Book Study Group |

- What were the book's most significant ideas and values to you as a teacher?
- What are the key themes and recurrent points in the book?
- Does anything in the book have meaning for your classroom or for the school?
- Did anything in the book lead you to reconsider your ideas about teaching and learning?
- Did anything in the book reinforce your ideas about teaching and learning?
- Have you previously used any of the book's ideas or strategies in your classroom and did you find them to be successful?

and the responsibilities of the individual assuming that role. It was emphasized that when serving as discussion leader it is important to remember that diversity in the level of understanding and outlook is what stimulates discussion, fosters learning, and keeps a book study group interesting.

The discussion leader's role is to ensure that the participants stay on topic, not to continually raise new questions or ideas, and to develop a list of questions to guide and stimulate conversation. To promote participation by all members of the group, the questions should be wide-ranging and rather broad. Several representative questions typically used are provided in Figure 5.3.

After further deliberation, the group mentioned above mutually agreed on the following leadership strategy for their meetings. Organizational arrangements and intergroup communication about each meeting would be facilitated by the staff developer. At the meetings, a different teacher, preferably on a volunteer basis, would be identified to serve as the discussion leader for the next book. The discussion leader's role would be to ensure that everyone got a chance to participate in the conversation, generate a list of discussion questions for the meeting, try to involve everyone, and research and make comments on the author's background.

Selecting Books for the Study Group

The most difficult aspect of the planning meeting was deciding how to choose the books to be read. The group set aside a lunchtime meeting at which the individual teachers would come prepared to recommend books for study and select books for the current semester of the school year. The staff developer was also asked to recommend a list of books to be considered by the group. It was agreed that the book list would be set by consensus.

Based on her experience with teacher book discussion groups, the staff developer made several suggestions regarding the selection of books and group activities.

- Select books that focus on educational issues in general.
- Each member of the group might read a different book on the same educational topic. The group could then compare and contrast the different authors' points of view.
- Choose a book that's relevant to the teaching and learning issues the teachers confront daily in their classrooms.
- Periodically read and discuss children's books and explore how they can be used to reinforce district standards.
- Occasionally bring a new voice to the conversation by inviting a college faculty member or an author to one of their meetings.
- Keep a journal reflecting on what has been read and what the group has discussed.

The staff developer suggested that the first book selected for study should be one that could be read in a reasonable period of time. This would allow the participating teachers, who lead complex professional lives, to discover the benefits of the book study group as quickly as possible. Additionally, she noted that the conversation that ensued during the initial group meetings was more likely to be lively and of substantial quality, to enhance the teachers' learning experience, and to help achieve whatever individual and group goals the teachers had for participating in the book study if they did not perceive the initial stages of the study group meetings to be burdensome. A form that can be used to plan study group meetings can be found in Figure 5.4.

These book club strategies encourage the teachers to analyze, compare, and contrast ideas, and they sustain the teachers' interest in book study. In this way, ongoing learning is promoted among members of the group. The case presented below highlights the activities of a meeting held by the group.

Case Study: A Teachers' Book Discussion Meeting

A group of teachers in a K–2 early childhood school voluntarily met on a regularly scheduled basis to read and discuss a professional book. The group consisted of six kindergarten teachers, three educational assistants, and a staff developer. Participation in the group was voluntary. The principal supported the group by funding the purchase of an adequate number of copies of the books that were selected for discussion by the group. Moreover,

Figure 5.4   Planning Guide for Study Group Meetings

I. Organizing the Meeting

a. Who should be involved in planning the first meeting of your study group?

_____

_____

_____

b. When and where should the initial planning meeting be held?

_____

_____

_____

c. Who are the potential members of the study group?

_____

_____

_____

d. What are the goals for the first planning meeting?

_____

_____

_____

e. What are the possible areas of study for the group?

_____

_____

_____

II. Resources Needed for the First Meeting

a. Do handouts need to be prepared for the first meeting? If so, what should be included?

_____

_____

_____

_____

b. Should the handouts be distributed during or prior to the meeting?

_____

_____

_____

c. Do the participants need to bring anything to the meeting (Example: test cores, other data, information on district or school initiatives, etc.)?

_____

_____

_____

d. What other materials/resources are needed for conducting the first planning meeting?

_____

_____

_____

(Continued)

Figure 5.4　Continued

III. Action Planning
What major steps do I need to take in order to implement this plan?

_____
_____
_____
_____

IV. Additional Notes

_____
_____
_____
_____
_____
_____
_____
_____

the principal often read the book under discussion and occasionally came to a meeting and participated in the conversation.

This group was currently focused on reading *Joyful Learning in Kindergarten* by Bobbi Fisher (1998). The teacher who was leading the discussion had distributed a list of discussion questions prior to the meeting. She opened the meeting by giving some information on the author's background and stimulated the conversation by soliciting responses to the discussion questions. The staff developer sometimes demonstrated specific instructional techniques relative to the ideas in the book and made recommendations for additional reading on points of interest to the study group participants. Some group members maintained reflective journals on their readings.

The meeting focused on a chapter in *Joyful Learning in Kindergarten* on shared reading. The discussion questions stimulated animated discussion about the ideas they had gotten out of the chapter. Participants related their experiences with shared reading in their own classrooms and made connections to the reading. There was a lot of interaction among staff members. Everyone participated, including the educational assistants. In response to one of the discussion questions, a teacher shared her reflections from her journal demonstrating that she was working on becoming a reflective practitioner. The staff developer facilitated the process by posing such questions as, *In what areas do you see shared reading working? Why did it work?*

The staff developer served as a resource for the teachers throughout the meeting. At one point, she did a demonstration of specific techniques for shared reading and also provided the participants with other literary resources for expanding their professional knowledge of reading. She showed how many of the ideas on shared reading that they discussed could be applied to guided reading. There was some discussion of a workshop on shared and guided reading that some of the participants were going to attend the next day. Other participants had attended similar workshops previously and shared what they had learned with their colleagues.

A major challenge for the group was finding a time to meet when everyone could get together without meeting after school. This was solved by scheduling meetings every other week during the teachers' planning periods. Initially, union concerns about the timing of the meetings were thought to be a potential obstacle for the group. Although the teachers were voluntarily meeting on their own time, the union felt that conducting meetings during teachers' planning periods was an abrogation of their contract. Some people who had been attending regularly stopped coming, because they did not want to be perceived as being in opposition to the union. However, a core group continued to participate because of their interest in the topic under study.

Despite the somewhat shaky start, the group was able to complete an in-depth study of the book over a period of three meetings. The discussion and the reflection that took place were very rewarding. The teachers and the principal liked the idea of providing a professional time to reflect on ideas concerning the teaching process. Educational assistants who attended the meetings took what they learned back to the classroom. The principal noticed subtle changes in instruction on the part of the participating teachers as well. Due to the success of this project, the plan is to select other books next year for this grade and to expand by starting a similar study group on another grade level.

CONCLUSION

Study groups serve as an important vehicle for building community. The success of study groups is dependent upon the support offered by the leaders of the school. They provide a job-embedded strategy for promoting collegiality among teachers.

6 Learning Through Classroom Observation

PREVIEW OF THE CHAPTER

As teachers plan for instruction, they characteristically focus on the materials, the content, and the activities associated with their teaching. Typically, they make instructional decisions in isolation from one another, guided primarily by school district policy, program mandates, and the expectations they hold for student achievement.

Teachers in learning community schools, however, place student learning at the core of their instructional planning and teaching practices. They consistently discuss instructional issues, share ideas, observe one another's teaching, and make plans to provide their students with meaningful content and authentic learning activities.

To transform their schools into learning communities, those in formal leadership positions must structure opportunities (a) for teachers to observe one another and receive constructive feedback from their peers and (b) for supervisors to observe teachers and engage them in mutually respectful dialogue about the observed teaching practices. Collegial classroom observation creates what we describe as a culture of collaborative instruction; that is, a culture in which teachers learn about learning by opening their classrooms up to supervisors and other teachers and routinely discuss observed teaching and learning behaviors. This chapter will focus on strategies for the observation of teaching behaviors that foster a culture of collaborative instruction. The chapter specifically addresses the following questions:

- What is the purpose of classroom observation?
- How does the standards-based walk-through for teachers contribute to a culture of collaborative instruction?
- How does conferencing with teachers set the stage for the classroom observation process?
- How does clinical supervision improve learning and foster collaboration?

WHAT IS THE PURPOSE OF CLASSROOM OBSERVATION?

Jack Somers, the principal of Elementary School #1 in the Menlo School District, has put several initiatives in place to promote faculty collegiality and to foster trust between the teachers and supervisors in his school. He recognizes that much must still be done to improve the learning opportunities offered to the students. At a recent meeting of the principal's cabinet, Mary Barry, his instructional supervisor, commented that many of the teachers were unresponsive to the written observation reports and the recommendations that she offers after observing their classes. They often seemed defensive and anxious during the planning and feedback conferences and uninterested in exploring any ideas that she might make for improving their lessons.

Mary noted that she had written a memo to the teachers informing them that she is willing to come into their classrooms and help them with any instructional issues they might want to address. Two of the new and inexperienced teachers welcomed her invitation, but she was disappointed by the overall lack of response from most of the staff. The other members of the cabinet agreed that although some steps had been taken to improve collegiality among the teachers, if instructional behavior is to improve, more must be done to encourage teachers to open their classrooms to one another and to make use of the instructional support and resources available from their supervisors. What supervisory strategies could they put into place to encourage teachers to open their classrooms for the observation process?

Teachers' Attitudes Toward Classroom Observation

The attitude of the teachers at Menlo School #1 toward classroom observation as experienced by their instructional supervisor, Mary Barry, is typical of what occurs all too often in our schools. We have found that this attitude has been shaped by several structural and cultural conditions. First, the culture of too many schools still considers the instruction as a professional activity that is carried out by teachers in isolation from one another. Second, most supervisors still do not routinely visit classrooms on an informal basis and provide teachers with feedback in a form that is useful. Classroom visitation is thereby perceived by teachers as an intrusion and as peripheral to the ongoing improvement of instruction. Third, policies and rules established in some schools and districts may make it uncomfortable for teachers to change their outlook on having frequent visitors in their classrooms. By way of example, we have found that teachers are often defensive because they believe that the presence of a supervisor in their classrooms indicates that they are being evaluated, as opposed to being offered support. Finally, supervisors and teachers have yet to learn to apply much of what is now known about how to improve learning. Given this environment, it is essential that all that teachers, supervisors, and administrators understand the purpose of the classroom visit and the conditions under which it can foster improved teaching and learning.

Purposes of Classroom Observation

Classroom observation, as discussed in this chapter, has as its fundamental purpose the gathering of information that teachers can use to learn about, reflect on, and improve their instructional behaviors (Sullivan & Glanz, 2000). As Sergiovanni (2001) points out that "it is difficult to justify any approach to supervision unless its primary emphasis is on teacher learning" (p. 267).

It is essential that both teachers and supervisors regularly engage in the observation of instruction. Classroom teachers should observe one another to foster a culture in which they collaborate, learn from one another, and construct shared pedagogical beliefs and strengths. The outcome is the building of community and a culture of collaborative instruction that fosters improved teaching and learning. The role of the instructional supervisor is to structure the observation process and serve as the facilitator, rather than to act as the arbiter of instruction.

Supervisors should routinely visit classrooms to identify teachers' needs and provide them with support. At the same time, it is equally as important for teachers to collaborate around observed teaching behavior.

Information Online 6.1

Study the Lesson Study Process

The lesson study is a collaborative and highly structured professional development strategy used by Japanese educators to reflect on their teaching behaviors and provide improved learning opportunities for their students. As part of the process, teachers collaboratively prepare, conduct, observe, analyze, and refine a set of lessons. To learn about the lesson study, visit the Website of the Lesson Study Research Group at http://www.tc.edu/centers/lessonstudy/lessonstudy.html

---

The Lesson Study: An Alternative Classroom Observation Strategy

Another popular classroom observation strategy that has emerged in the literature is the lesson study. It builds community in schools by allowing teachers to come together to plan lessons that enhance student and teacher learning. Information about the lesson study can be found in Information Online 6.1.

HOW DOES THE STANDARDS-BASED WALK-THROUGH FOR TEACHERS CONTRIBUTE TO A CULTURE OF COLLABORATIVE INSTRUCTION?

A strategy that lends itself to promoting a culture of collaborative instruction is the *standards-based walk-through*, a structured process we use for opening up classrooms so that educators can observe one another and learn from what occurs in other classrooms. It has as its focus the nurturing of collaboration around the content standards adopted by the participating schools and districts. The standards-based walk-through is unique in that we have structured it to be planned and carried out solely by teachers.

Several well-structured protocols for conducting walk-throughs are discussed in the literature. Various models and materials have been developed to serve different purposes and different audiences. For example, the Lesley University Literacy Collaborative has prepared a user-friendly walk-through guide for principals and literacy coordinators that has literacy teaching and the physical organization of classrooms as its focus.

In another model, the LearningWalk^sm, developed by the Institute for Learning at the University of Pittsburg, a team of educators and others concerned about learning use a structured process to walk about the school observing the practice of teaching and learning. They visit classrooms, converse with students, and make note of the quality of the learning experiences offered by the school. They conclude the walk by providing feedback to the principal that can be shared and reflected on with teachers and other staff members (Institute of Learning, 1998).

For any walk-through process to achieve its goals, it is necessary that the participants have the structure, knowledge, and communication skills needed to carry out the process. A process used for conducting the standards-based walk-through is provided in the sections that follow.

The Standards-Based Walk-Through Process for Teachers

The protocol that we have developed, the *standards-based walk-through*, provides for an organized tour of the building by teams of teachers, who visit their peers' classrooms; observe the classroom environment and learning centers; review student work samples, special projects, and portfolios; and examine other classroom artifacts that the teacher has put on display for the walk-through. Barth (1990) has pointed out that

> teachers also need to be able to relate their classroom behavior to what other teachers are doing in their classrooms. Teachers think they do that. Many do, but many do not do it very systematically or regularly. (p. 49)

The standards-based walk-though is unique precisely because it does focus on enabling teachers to learn by exploring and relating to what other teachers are doing in their classrooms. Because it is designed and carried out by teachers, it helps to develop their leadership capacity among members of the teaching staff. We have structured the process so that neither students nor supervisors are present during the walk.

Content Standards and the Standards-Based Walk-Through

Our model of the walk-through is driven by the implementation of the content standards that have been adopted by school districts. This does not preclude a school from using the process to focus on other areas of interest. We initiated the process because building principals, with whom we were working, were struggling to identify ways of getting teachers to become comfortable with and respond to the standards that had been mandated as the focus of instruction in their districts.

Clearly, instructional practice and educational reform efforts have been profoundly influenced by the standards movement. Standards provide teachers with a blueprint for setting goals, planning curriculum, identifying effective instructional strategies, and assessing student performance. Once standards have been set, if teachers are to know what to do with them, they need ongoing direction and adequate support. We view the school walk-through as a strategy that serves this purpose by permitting teachers to observe their colleagues' work in relation to the standards as they seek ways of improving learning opportunities for their students.

Purposes and Outcomes of the Walk

The tour is conducted on a professional development day when the students are not present in the school building. The purposes for teachers are to

- Look for evidence of activities that reflect the implementation of the district's content standards in the classroom.
- Review materials and products and learn from the classroom practices of their peers.
- Engage in an activity around classroom practice and instructional materials that can serve as a basis for in-depth discussion and the exchange of ideas.
- Cultivate classroom observation as an aspect of their roles as leaders.
- Learn what students in other grades are expected to know and what activities and projects are used to help achieve the standards.
- Enhance their leadership capacity.

Tips for planning and conducting a successful standards-based walk-through are provided in Figure 6.1.

What Teams Do During the Standards-Based Walk-Through

During the walk-through, the team members visit the classrooms to which they have been assigned and record their observations on a documentation form (see Figure 6.2 on pg. 125). They review student work for evidence of standards-related activities. They identify instructional activities, teacher-made instructional materials, and learning centers that might have implications for standards-based teaching in their own classrooms. They look for instructional activities that develop students' higher-level thinking skills. They make note of the layout of classrooms and content of bulletin boards and other displays in the classroom. If they are available,

Figure 6.1	Tips for Conducting a Standards-Based Walk-Through
Who participates in the Standards-Based walk-through?	All teachers in the school participate walk-through. The teachers are organized in teams of two to three teachers from one grade level. If necessary, the size of the team can be adjusted based on the number of teachers in the school. Home room teachers are never in their classrooms during the visit.
Which classrooms will the teams of teachers visit?	A walk-through is generally organized so that the teams from one grade level observe the classrooms of teachers from other grade levels. Early childhood teachers who visit upper-grade classes report that, in addition to the other benefits of the walk-through, they obtain some perspective about the content that they are preparing their students to master in subsequent years.
What materials must be prepared prior to the walk-through?	An agenda detailing the visitation process and activities and a school walk-through documentation form must be prepared prior to the classroom visits. The agenda should be distributed in advance and should include the following: • The room in which the faculty will meet on the day of the walk-through for an overview of the planned activities. • A visitation schedule listing the members of each team and the rooms and times at which they are to visit. • The room and time at which teachers are to report for grade-level dialogue after the walk-through is completed.
What do classroom teachers do to prepare for other teachers to walk through their classrooms?	The classroom teacher should put on display instructional material that reflect classroom activities relating to the implementation of the standards, including student work samples, portfolios, writing folders, special projects, learning center, books, and other reading materials. The teachers may also want to make lesson plans available for review.
What is the instructional focus of the classroom visit?	The walk-through is viewed through the prism of the district's content standards. Teachers may decide to address a particular aspect of the content standards. A documentation form, which is distributed to the teachers at the information session, will indicate the focus of the walk-through. A sample form is provided in Figure 6.4.

visitors may also review the teacher's lesson plans to see the scope and sequence used by the teacher for standards-related instructional planning.

As a team of teachers reviews the various artifacts in the classrooms, they share their perceptions with each other. However, as instructed in the meeting held prior to the walk-through, they do not evaluate; rather, they describe what they see that reflects the implementation of the standards and effective educational practice.

What Teams Do After the Walk-Through

After the walk-through, the teachers attend grade-level meetings to discuss their observations and responses to the items on the documentation form. Finally, they prepare a brief summary sheet listing (a) the things that they learned about standards-based teaching and learning as found in their notes, and (b) the ideas they would like to replicate in their own classrooms. All summary sheets are then submitted to the principal and a brief report, indicating what the teachers have learned from the process, is prepared for dissemination to the faculty.

The walk-through, in addition to contributing to the building of community, is structured to provide for a cross-fertilization of ideas from teachers at all grade levels. In this one professional activity, they have the opportunity to share expertise and acquire new knowledge in three settings: (1) when dialoguing in teams of two or three, (2) when meeting with all the teachers on their grade level, and (3) when they observe in the classrooms of teachers from other grade levels. The strategy permits every teacher in the school to provide learning opportunities for their peers, and the final report provides concrete evidence that they can learn from one another. As one teacher wrote,

> I always look forward to the walk-through. We now walk through twice a year and most of the teachers enjoy the process and learn a lot. It makes me feel good about being a teacher. The walk-through lets me see the teachers in my school in a different light. I am always surprised at the creative ways I see of teaching to and rein-forcing the standards. I am motivated to try new things with my class when I see how innovative some of the teachers can be. After our last walk-through, a teacher from another grade level, whom I don't know too well, asked if she could come to my room to discuss how I used some of the instructional materials that I had made. I think the school walk-through is one of the better ideas that the principal has introduced to our school.

Figure 6.2	Standards-Based Walk-Through Documentation Form

Focus of the Visit: _____Content Standards in Literacy and Mathematics_____

Classroom:_____   **Team Members:**_____

Guiding Questions:

- What evidence did you see of the implementation of literacy standards in the classrooms you visited?
- What evidence did you see of the implementation of mathematics standards in the classrooms you visited?
- What evidence did you see of standards related outcomes in the classrooms you visited?
- What student work samples, projects, or portfolio artifacts did you see that you might replicate with your students?
- What instructional strategies did you see evidence of that you might use in your classroom?
- What materials did you observe that you might find useful for your students?
- What questions did this walk-through bring to the surface that need further clarification?

Summary Sheet:

- Summarize the new things learned by your team during the walk-through and list the ideas you might implement in your classroom.

HOW DOES CONFERENCING WITH TEACHERS SET THE STAGE FOR THE CLASSROOM OBSERVATION PROCESS?

Whereas strategies such as the walk-through and the lesson study focus on collaborative interaction among teachers, conferencing strategies have as their focal point the planned interaction that occurs between teachers and their supervisors. Conferencing with teachers is an important aspect of the classroom observation process that permits teachers and supervisors to work together on mutually agreed-upon objectives, and it can contribute to improved learning for both teachers and students. Leaders of learning communities can set the stage for implementing a successful collegial classroom observation program in three arenas: (a) at the annual conference with the entire teaching staff at the beginning of the school year; (b) at articulation conferences conducted with each teacher at the beginning

Information Online 6.2

Conducting a Walk-Through

To learn about the processes and procedures used by a school district to conduct walk-throughs, read the article *Face to Face* (Barnes, Miller & Dennis, 2001), available at http://www.nscd.org/library/jsd/barnes224.html

and end of the school year; and (c) at planning and feedback conferences held before and after classroom instruction. The conferences can be used to promote and reinforce a school's shared vision, to foster collegiality among teachers and supervisors, and to provide learning opportunities for the staff. The use of effective communication skills, both verbal and nonverbal, is essential if those in leadership positions are to conduct successful meetings (see Chapter 2). Strategies for conducting each type of conference are discussed below.

Faculty Conference at the Beginning of the School Year

At the beginning of the school year, the principal should conduct a schoolwide faculty conference. This meeting should include discussion of two important issues: developing a shared understanding of the school's classroom observation process and developing shared beliefs about what constitutes effective instruction (see Figure 6.3).

Developing a Shared Understanding of the Observation Process

At the faculty conference, the purposes for conducting classroom visits should be openly discussed. Teachers and supervisors should be encouraged to talk about what they expect from classroom visits. We have found that this strategy helps to remove the threat that is often associated with classroom visits from supervisors. The following journal excerpt describes what was experienced by a new teacher in a school in which one of the writers served as a facilitator:

> As a new teacher, I became anxious when my supervisor informed me that he would pay a visit to my classroom within the next week

---

Figure 6.3   Sharing a Vision of the Observation Process

Teachers and supervisors must have

- A shared vision of what effective teaching looks like.
- A shared understanding of the elements of the observation process that is used in the school. Teachers should know what to expect when a supervisor enters the classroom.

Supervisors and administrators must

- Communicate to teachers that supervision is a process for the improvement of instruction.
- Understand what teachers need and expect from the observation process.

---

to see how I was doing. Previously, he had told me to let him know if I needed any help with the curriculum. Although I felt that I could use some support, I wasn't certain how I could ask for it without seeming incompetent. I didn't want to be thought of as one of the "weak" teachers in the school. I asked some of the other teachers what happened when the supervisor came to observe, but I got different responses from the three teachers that I spoke to. I couldn't get a clear picture of what to expect. This only added to my anxiety about the upcoming observation.

The above excerpt is typical of what too many teachers experience. Lacking a shared understanding of what is to occur, they tend to perceive a visit as a judgmental activity that surfaces their own concerns about their instructional skills and is influenced by their interpersonal rapport and relationship with the supervisor. Teachers are more likely to perceive the observations as collegial when the process is discussed openly with the principal and other supervisors and when they are offered the opportunity to shape the process to fit their needs.

Developing Shared Beliefs About Effective Teaching

Teachers and supervisors should also hold shared beliefs about what effective instructional practice looks like. These shared understandings guide teachers as they collegially select instructional activities for their students. Facultywide conversation that addresses instructional practice builds community and communicates that those in leadership positions see teachers as a source of expertise about teaching and learning.

Individual Conferences With Teachers at the Beginning and End of the School Year

One–on-one conferences held with teachers provide supervisors with the opportunity to build collegial relationships with teachers. Ideally, the building principal should hold individual conferences with each teacher at the beginning and the end of each school year. If the staff is too large, the meetings can be conducted by each teacher's instructional supervisor. During the first meeting, the teacher and supervisor should analyze the achievement data for the teacher's new class, and the supervisor should elicit from the teacher the instructional areas that should receive special attention during the school year. A similar meeting, held at the end of the year, affords teachers the opportunity to discuss the year's accomplishments and to share what they have learned form the year's work.

The following strategies for conducting individual conferences with teachers are suggested.

Plan to conduct the conferences about three weeks into the new school year. This will give teachers time to prepare by reviewing achievement data, observing their students, and conducting assessments to identify their students' needs. The end of the year conference should be held in June. To set the stage for a collegial tone during the meeting, notify the teachers in sufficient time so that they can have time to prepare for the meeting.

Prepare an agenda for the meeting. Figure 6.4 lists some suggested topics for the agenda. The list, which is not exhaustive, includes items that may be primary discussion topics for teachers, supervisors, or both teachers and supervisors. We believe that the focus of the conference should be directed toward student learning and suggest that it include a review of the achievement data of the students in the teacher's class. Teachers should be encouraged to discuss the needs of individual students so as to communicate that student academic growth and development is always the central focus of the learning community. The agenda items suggested for the end-of-the-year conference afford the teacher and the supervisor the opportunity to assess, reflect back, and identify the learning strategies that resulted in improved teaching and learning for the various members of the school community.

Send a copy of the agenda to all teachers prior to the conferences. This will eliminate the element of surprise, relieve anxiety, enable teachers to come to the meeting prepared to engage in a dialogue, maintain rapport, and foster a collegial tone throughout the discussion.

Open each conference by going over the agenda items, sharing your objectives for the conference, and asking about the teacher's objectives for the meeting. It is important that teachers experience some sense of control

Figure 6.4	Suggested Agenda Items for Individual Conference With Teachers

Beginning-of-Year Conference	End-of-Year Conference
Teacher	
Preferred teaching style	Reflections on student learning
Expectations for supervisory process	Reflections on personal learning
Expectations for student achievement	Reflections on supervisory activities
Supervisor	
District objectives/plan for school year	Review of district objectives/plans
Schoolwide objectives	Review of schoolwide objectives
	Reflection on personal learning
Teacher and Supervisor	
Review and analysis of student data	Review of year-end student data
Review of effective teaching practices	Learning activities for teachers for the coming school year
Expectations for grade-level/planning periods Informal visitations and feedback	Other topics of interest or concern
Formal observation process	
Other topics of interest or concern	

over the process if professionalism and collaboration are to be fostered. Encourage teachers to reflect on the instructional decisions that they have made for the school year. As you address each agenda item, remember that the primary focus should be on teacher expectations for student learning, as student learning is the focus of all learning community activities. Remember also to address teacher learning. Inform teachers of the professional learning opportunities that will be available for them throughout the school year.

Close the conference held at the beginning of the school year by summarizing and making notes on the results of the discussion. Keep notes on all meetings held with each teacher throughout the year. At the end-of-the-year conference, you will have a running record of all meetings held with each teacher, which can contribute to the process of reflection.

Conducting Planning and Feedback Conferences With Teachers

Throughout the school year, supervisors should hold planning conferences with teachers prior to conducting classroom observations. These conferences provide teachers with the opportunity to reflect on and share with supervisors information about the uniqueness of their classrooms and the instructional outcomes and strategies that they have selected for the lesson that is to be observed.

The supervisor should clarify the focus of the lesson and review the specific logistics that are to be followed including the time and place of the observation, the data-collection procedures, and plans for a follow-up conference. The planning conference can be used to establish a sense of collegiality and cooperation in achieving specific instructional outcomes, to reduce the teacher's anxiety, and to build confidence and trust in the process (Acheson & Gall, 1997).

Feedback conferences should be held after a classroom observation to afford the teacher the opportunity to analyze the lesson and to provide feedback to the teacher (Acheson & Gall, 1997). The logistics for conducting these planning and feedback conferences are described in a section below.

HOW DOES CLINICAL SUPERVISION IMPROVE LEARNING AND FOSTER COLLABORATION?

In any school, attempts to improve and increase the learning opportunities for students will depend on the availability of high-quality learning opportunities for teachers and supervisors. Supervisors, as the "lead learners" in their schools, must establish a framework that encourages teachers to talk to them openly and comfortably about their observed teaching practices. Classroom observation processes must be conducted in a context that enables the participants to freely analyze what occurs in the classroom and to generate strategies that lead to an improvement in instruction. Clinical supervision is a strategy that sets the stage for communication between teachers and supervisors in the classroom observation process.

Defining Clinical Supervision

The study of clinical supervision as a method for analyzing observed teaching behavior has its roots in the work of Goldhammer (1969), Cogan (1973), and other researchers who were searching for techniques to produce solidly prepared candidates for the teaching profession. Cogan (1973) precisely describes clinical supervision as

> the rationale and practice designed to improve the teacher's classroom performance. It takes its principal data from the events of the classroom. The analysis of these data and the relationship between

teacher and supervisor form the basis of the program, procedures and strategies designed to improve the teacher's classroom behavior. (p. 9)

Acheson and Gall (1997) identify the following three steps in the clinical supervision process: (1) the planning conference, (2) classroom observation and data collection, and (3) the feedback conference.

Clinical supervision is meant to be a cyclical process. The teacher and supervisor are to work together, repeating the series of three steps in the cycle so as to enhance the teacher's skills. As Acheson and Gall (1997) point out, the importance placed on the teacher-supervisor relationship and the opportunity for the growth are the most significant aspects of the model.

Strategies for Promoting Learning
During the Planning Conference

Teachers report that they often experience a great deal of professional dissatisfaction and anxiety during and after conferences held to plan for a supervisory visit to their classrooms. All too often, the supervisor takes the lead and controls the content of these planning meetings. A teacher wrote movingly about a recent planning conference held with her supervisor.

> My assistant principal conducted our conference just as she always does. I had been informed she would visit my class during my language arts lesson the following Wednesday. At her request, I answered questions about what I planned to teach and what I hoped to accomplish with my students during the lesson. After making some comments about my progress through the curriculum, she told me what she expected to see during her visit, indicating that it would require some changes in the planned lesson. Lastly, she asked if I had any questions about the observation. I didn't raise any questions because I was relieved that the meeting had come to an end. My supervisor knows that I have some unresolved discipline issues in my classroom, so our meetings always make me feel uneasy. I know that the discipline issue is always just below the surface any time that we talk about my class. Her "I question and you answer" conferences don't help the situation. As usual, when I left her office, I felt like one of my sixth-grade students rather than like a teacher.

The demeanor exhibited by the supervisor in this conference is not likely to create confidence or a sense of collegiality in the teacher or a culture of collaborative instruction. Clinical supervision, which has the goal of helping teachers to improve their instructional performance, calls for a more collegial approach to conferencing. In the clinical cycle, the supervisor is called upon to facilitate the following behaviors when conducting a planning conference. These behaviors foster teacher and supervisor learning and the building of community.

1. Collaboratively identify the instructional issues that are of concern to the teacher and the aspects of the lesson that the teacher wants to be the focus of the observation. (Acheson & Gall, 1997.)

2. Listen closely to the teacher. Utilize effective communication strategies to cultivate and maintain a collaborative teacher-supervisor relationship. (See Chapter 2.)

3. Maintain a collegial environment that permits the teacher to review, discuss, and, if necessary, refine the planned lesson.

4. Mutually agree on a strategy for collecting information during the observation. (Acheson & Gall, 1997.)

5. Jointly make logistical decisions about such issues as the role of the supervisor and the time, place, and length of the observation and the feedback conference. (Acheson & Gall, 1997; Goldhammer, Anderson, & Krajewski, 1993).

Strategies for the Classroom Observation

The observation of the lesson should be scheduled to occur shortly after the planning conference. To maintain the trust that is an important aspect of learning community schools, the supervisor should adhere to the behaviors agreed-upon during the planning meeting (Acheson & Gall, 1997; Goldhammer et al., 1993).

An example is provided below.

During a planning meeting, John, a teacher at Menlo School #1, has indicated that he is concerned about the clarity of the directions that he gives to his students. Some students frequently fail to follow his directions. He also believes that he spends an undue amount of valuable time responding to questions about the directions that he has given to the class. Initially, he assumed that the students were not listening attentively to his directions. Now, he is beginning to wonder if his questions may contribute the problem.

After some discussion of the issue with Mary Barry, his supervisor, it was mutually agreed that she would conduct a series of data-collection

---

Information Online 6.3

To learn more about data collection strategies visit the Website http://linguistics.byu.edu/classes/ling577lh/Eyes.html. It describes six data-collection procedures (selective verbatim, verbal flow, at-task class traffic, interaction analysis, and global scan) that are part of an Association for Supervision and Curriculum Development (ASCD) video program, *Another Pair of Eyes.*

---

visits to his classroom on dates that they selected. On the first visit, Mary quietly entered the classroom and made a written record of all of the directions he gave to the class. She also listed any questions that the students asked to clarify the meaning of his questions. Mary used an audiotape machine to supplement her written record, to which the teacher had agreed during the planning conference. At the close of the lesson, she left the room quietly.

In the above scenario, the written report should be free of inferences and value judgments, and should record word-for-word the teacher's directions and the students' queries about the teacher's directions. The collection of objective data is critical in the observation process. Unbiased data increase the probability that teachers will develop an accurate view of their behaviors, the behaviors of their students, and of what is transpiring in their classrooms (Acheson & Gall, 1997; Goldhammer et al., 1980).

Strategies for Conducting the Feedback Conference

During the feedback conference, the supervisor strives to create a supportive environment and to provide the teacher with useful information. Collegiality and cooperation should be the keynotes of the conference. The teacher should be encouraged to discuss, explain, and analyze the data gathered during the observation. The points listed below should be included in the process (Acheson & Gall, 1997; Daresh & Playko, 1995):

- The teacher should be encouraged to analyze what the data indicate has occurred during the lesson. The supervisor's role is to provide clarification. Analyzing means "simply describing what the recorded information shows is happening without making value judgments" (Acheson & Gall, 1997).

- Encourage the teacher to explore the implications of the data. This promotes reflection and learning. If a decision is made to modify or change behavior, the supervisor helps the teacher to come up with some strategies that might be worth trying out.
- Each feedback session should conclude with some agreed upon plans for improvement and a date for a follow-up meeting.

For example:

On Friday, Carol, a teacher in Elementary School #1 in the Menlo School District, had a planning meeting with her instructional supervisor, Mary Barry. It was agreed that during her observation, data would be collected on her use of questions and that they would meet on Wednesday to discuss the data. On the Monday following the observation, Mary gave Carol a list of the questions so that she could review them and be prepared for their feedback conference.

By capturing only the data that was agreed upon in their planning meeting and giving it to Carol prior to their feedback session, Mary has set the stage for a tension-free conference.

Clinical Supervision as a Learning Strategy

In learning community schools, we view each stage of the clinical supervision process as a strategy for promoting learning for both teachers and supervisors. It is the role of supervisors to make teachers aware of the new knowledge that is acquired as they move through each stage of the process.

During the planning conference, as the teacher describes the lesson to be presented, the supervisor learns more about the teacher's instructional practice, preferences, and needs. The teacher acquires new ideas about how to conduct the planned lesson as it is discussed and analyzed. During the observation process, supervisors learn about the teacher's skill as an instructor and rapport with students. During the feedback conference, through a process of describing what has occurred, questioning and discussing the teaching techniques, and reflecting on student outcomes and strategies for improvement, the knowledge base for both teachers and supervisors is expanded. The dialogue that occurs should be directed toward fostering a deeper understanding of the practices that promote improved learning opportunities for students. Supervisors must be mindful that the learning must be recognized and articulated if the clinical process is to nurture a culture of collaborative instruction between both parties.

During the clinical cycle, we encourage supervisor to make use of a set of research-based feedback strategies that have been demonstrated to be effective either as part of or apart from conferences held with teachers. In research on teachers' perception of effective principal-teacher interaction, Blase and Blase (1999) identified five "talking strategies" that principals used to encourage teacher reflection: (1) making suggestions for improving instruction, (2) giving feedback about observed instruction, (3) modeling teaching techniques followed by discussion, (4) asking for advice and opinions about teaching and instructional programs, and (5) praising particular teaching strategies. These talking strategies are linked to the development of learning communities because they encourage reflective teacher behavior, promote a focus on student learning, and provide learning opportunities for teachers. Specific information on the communication techniques needed to carry out the strategies is provided in Chapter 2.

CONCLUSION

Clinical supervision is a strategy that not only provides teachers with a nonthreatening climate for examining and improving their teaching behaviors, but also serves to cultivate and sustain the development of a school as a learning community. A number of writers (Acheson & Gall, 1997 Sergiovanni, 2001; Sullivan & Glanz, 2000) have associated the learning community characteristics of collaboration and collegiality with the practice of clinical supervision. Sullivan and Glanz (2000) have extended the clinical supervision cycle to include a reflective practice phrase.

Our practice and analysis of the clinical supervision process confirms that each step in the cycle affords the supervisor an opportunity to reinforce a school's transformation into a learning community. During planning conferences, the supervisor creates a nonthreatening environment that fosters a culture of collegiality and promotes the sharing of leadership by letting the teacher determine the focus and logistics of the planned observation. As teachers become more and more comfortable with the presence of an observer in the classroom, a climate supporting the deprivatization of practice is fostered. During feedback conferences, the teacher and observer collaboratively reflect on the teacher's instructional practices as the teacher is guided to reach conclusions about any needed changes. Over time, the hierarchical relationship that usually characterizes interactions between a teacher and supervisor is replaced by a collaborative work style. Most importantly, the process results in both parties learning more about teaching and learning.

7 Learning Through Collaborative Approaches

Assessment of Student Work, Mentoring, Diversity, and Parental Involvement

PREVIEW OF THE CHAPTER

Collaboration is the vital factor in the development and maintenance of professional learning communities. Without collaboration, there would be no learning communities. This chapter continues the discussion of collaborative approaches for improving instruction. It examines collaborative assessment of student work, mentoring, and parental involvement and touches on issues of equity and diversity in collaboration. The questions it seeks to answer are these:

- What is the role of collaboration in the learning community?
- How does collaborative assessment of student work build learning communities?
- How does mentoring enhance the learning community?

- How may issues of equity and diversity be addressed in a collaborative learning community?
- How may we collaborate with parents in the learning community?

WHAT IS THE ROLE OF COLLABORATION IN THE LEARNING COMMUNITY?

Let's look in on Pat Martin, a new teacher in the Menlo School District. It is the day before school officially opens, and we find him sitting alone in his classroom. During the past few days he has attended the orientation program for new teachers run by the district, as well as the one in his school. They were well run, and he got helpful information and a lot of material from them. A teacher has been assigned to be his "buddy" through the first weeks of school.

Although he is very enthusiastic, Pat is feeling a little uncertain as he is about to face his very own class for the first time. His anxieties are related to the act of actually teaching. He has so many questions. What is the best way to teach the reading program the school requires? How will I know if my students are really learning?

"Teaching is really so isolated," he thinks to himself. "I'll be here in my classroom alone with my kids with no one to advise me or give me a thumbs up or a nudge when I'm about to fall on my face. There's no real time to exchange ideas with colleagues, except when I can grab them in the faculty room at lunch time or during my prep period. It would be so great to have someone with whom to bounce around ideas about instruction."

Just then, there is a light tap on his door. He looks up to see Mrs. Diaz and Mr. Patel, who both teach the same grade as Pat.

"Hi. How's it going?" Mrs. Diaz glances at the pile of books on Pat's desk. "Feeling a little overwhelmed?"

"Don't worry. It's not as bad as it looks," interjects Mr. Patel. "We'll be able to help you through it. The four of us on this grade meet regularly during our prep time and sometimes at lunch to plan units and talk about teaching strategies. We'd be happy to have you join us."

"Yes," adds Mrs. Diaz. "We're a friendly group, although sometimes the discussions can get hot and heavy. The bottom line is that we all have the children's learning at heart and that's what keeps us coming back. In fact, we'll be getting together this afternoon at 12:30 in my room. Come on over."

Pat breaks into a grin as relief floods over him. Suddenly, he does not feel alone anymore. He eagerly accepts their invitation and, as we leave Pat, he is chatting comfortably with his new colleagues.

The feeling of isolation that Pat experienced is all too often the lot of teachers. His initial thoughts reflect the traditional staff experience, in which they come together at faculty meetings usually focused on administrative issues, but essentially work in isolation. Through collaboration, groups of teachers work together for the improvement of instruction. They are thus able to bring their diverse viewpoints, skills, and experiences to the teaching and learning process. Collaboration is a vital factor in building and maintaining a community of learners. The essence of learning communities is people working together for improved student outcomes. Collaboration in learning communities takes many forms. Collaborative assessment of student work and mentoring are two of them. Issues of equity and diversity often emerge during collaboration and should be addressed collaboratively. In addition, staff collaborates with the families of students. In the following discussion, we examine each of these aspects of collaboration.

HOW DOES COLLABORATIVE ASSESSMENT OF STUDENT WORK BUILD LEARNING COMMUNITIES?

Assessing student work has traditionally been a significant responsibility of a teacher. Usually, this is done by the teacher working alone. Recently, however, there has been an increased interest in looking at student work together. Jointly assessing student work is one of the most effective ways to focus attention on student learning, and it is a powerful factor in developing and maintaining a professional learning community. Some of the purposes are to enhance professional development, to determine the effectiveness of teaching practices and the curriculum, to set standards, and, ultimately, to promote improved student performance (Cushman, 1996; Richardson, 2001a).

There are many benefits to this approach. It helps teachers to focus on the results of their instruction; it provides a vehicle for conversations on teaching and learning based on reality, not just theory; and it is an extremely effective professional development approach.

An Example

Looking at student work together may be done at any grade level. The most memorable experience one of the authors had in collaborative

---

Tips for Leaders 7.1

Plan Ahead

Make preparations for looking at student work. Decide how the samples will be displayed so that everyone can see them comfortably. Remove or cover pupil names. If copies have to be made, be sure that there are enough for everyone. If the student work requires special equipment, such as a VCR for a videotape, check that it is available and working. In addition, make other meeting preparations as outlined in Chapter 4.

---

examination of student work was with a group of prekindergarten and kindergarten teachers. We were trying to link our instruction to the district goals and were struggling with designing assessment assignments that were developmentally appropriate for the young children. For this discussion, we selected one of the math goals, and each teacher brought three levels of work. The range of activities represented in the work samples for the same goal was amazing. They included hands-on activities and paper-and-pencil work. The discussion was very animated as teachers debated what these works showed about young children's thinking, and queried one another as to the assignments and about the instructional activities leading up to them.

This was the first time this faculty had looked at student work together, and they were very enthusiastic about the experience. What was even more memorable was that, in the weeks that followed, we observed teachers incorporating some of the assessment assignments that were more developmentally appropriate into their classroom practices. This was evidence of ongoing learning on the part of the staff, an important characteristic of a professional learning community. This showed how collaborative examination of student work can help improve instruction and help build a learning community, even at the earliest level.

Several principles underlie collaborative examination of student work. It gives important information about the effectiveness of instruction in a learning community, and it should be made public (Annenberg Institute for School Reform, 2001). This does not mean, however, that an individual student's work should be identified; it means that the products of education should be available for examination. The schoolwork of students is

Figure 7.1	Assessing Student Work	
	Traditional Approach	*Collaborative Approach*
Who	The teacher working alone	The teacher and others working jointly
What	Each piece of student work	A few samples of student work
Why	Mainly to assess individual student progress	For many reasons: for example, to assess and inform curriculum and instructional practices and for professional development
When	Whenever convenient for the individual teacher	Has to be scheduled with others: Sufficient time must be allowed for examination, reflection, and discussion

important and it can take many forms. It may be paper-and-pencil work; it may take the form of an art object or a musical or dramatic presentation, depending on the assignment. Standards should be considered in any discussion or examination of student work. Therefore, assignments given the students for this process should be in accordance with the school, district, or state standards, as in the example presented earlier. Collaborative examination of student work over a period of time helps teachers monitor the relationships between student performance and changes in instructional strategies or curriculum (Annenberg Institute for School Reform, 2001).

The collaborative approach does not necessarily replace the day-to-day assessment of individual student work by the classroom teacher working alone. There are differences in the procedures and the purposes. These are summarized in Figure 7.1.

Making It Work: Strategies for Success

It's not enough just to pull teachers together, give them a pile of student work, and say, "Let's look at these and discuss them." Research has revealed several approaches that promote success in collaborative examination of student work (Richardson, 2001a, 2001b). Some of them are summarized below.

- Create a school culture in which teachers feel comfortable about commenting about one another's student work and don't feel threatened by having their own pupils' work discussed publicly

---

Tips for Leaders 7.2

Off to the Best Start

When you are just beginning to look at student work collaboratively in your school, consider having an outside facilitator who is experienced in this approach work with your groups to help develop their skills and get them started.

See Chapters 2 and 9 for more on the culture of the learning community.

- Provide teachers with the skills and the tools for this work. The group process skills discussed in Chapter 4 and specific strategies for looking at student work should be part of their professional repertoire.
- Set aside time for this experience. Some schools schedule two hours a week; others may do it during a professional day.
- Rotate leadership so that all participants have a chance to be in charge of the process.
- Recruit volunteers. Teachers are more enthusiastic and motivated when they select to engage in the process than when participation is mandatory.
- Include specialists and other teachers, such as bilingual and special education teachers, in the process. They are often able to offer a unique perspective to the group.
- Call in experts and provide other resources to the groups when needed. Although most of the discussion and reflection is among the staff members themselves, there may be times when outside specialists are required.
- Use a systematic approach to looking at student work together. Protocols facilitate the process and enhance productivity. If not using a protocol, decide on another system.

A protocol provides guidelines and a framework for looking at and discussing student work, and it fosters more effective use of time. There are several types of protocols for different purposes. For example, one model is designed to give teachers feedback on authentic assessment, and another model is designed for examining and upgrading the quality of instruction (Richardson, 2001c). Because there are many protocols, the group must define its purpose before choosing one.

Information Online 7.1

For more information on collaborative examination of student work, visit the Looking at Student Work Website of the Annenberg Institute for School Reform at http://www.lasw.org.

Getting Started

Now that you have decided to look at student work together, how do you actually get started? Here are some suggestions and tips garnered from our own experiences and the literature (Annenberg Institute for School Reform, 2001; Cushman, 1996; Richardson, 2001b).

- *Pick a method.* It is imperative that the group select or develop a process by which to examine student work. Sufficient time should be spent on discussing the reasons for using a particular method or protocol.
- *Relate to goals and standards.* One way to get started is to select a specific area of student performance related to a district or school standard or goal. The type of work collected should demonstrate in a meaningful way the students' performance in relationship to the standard, as in the example previously presented.
- *Decide on the types of work to study.* It could be projects, art, written work, or other products.
- *Collect student samples.* It is best to have work from a range of abilities. Work samples that reflect various levels of student performance stimulate more meaningful discussion. The wide range of work samples was one of the reasons the conversation among the early childhood teachers mentioned previously was so enlivened.
- *Have a central question.* It helps to get discussion started and keeps it on track if there is a central question. Examples of such questions are, *What evidence is there in the student work of applying scientific knowledge? To what degree do these student products demonstrate an understanding of area and perimeter? What strengths and weakness do these student samples show?*

Here are some tips for what to do when examining student work collaboratively:

- Ask your colleagues questions about any aspect of the sample or the assignment you don't understand.

- Try to see what and how the student was thinking while creating the work.
- Identify how the student samples relate to the curriculum standards.
- Reflect on insights the samples raise about instruction, assignments, and assessment procedures.
- Keep an open mind to your colleagues' views.
- Express your own ideas clearly.
- Think about the implications that the samples and the discussion have for your own instructional practices. In the example presented, many of the teachers applied ideas in their own classrooms that they had gained from looking at student work together.
- Reflect on the process and whether the method or protocol selected was effective.

HOW DOES MENTORING ENHANCE THE LEARNING COMMUNITY?

Many schools have moved away from the informal buddy system that Pat had and into a formal mentoring program for new teachers. The frequency with which new teachers leave during or just after their first year and the large numbers of teachers who are protected to retire make it imperative that schools adopt strong support systems for inexperienced teachers. Demographic changes and the increasing diversity of our student population pose additional challenges to the new teacher. Many states require mentoring programs for new teachers, and major teacher organizations advocate this as well (Portner, 1998). In order to maintain a learning community, new teachers must not only be supported in the development of their instructional and management skills, but must also be assimilated into the culture of the school. Mentoring is therefore a necessary element of a professional learning community.

Mentorship brings many benefits to the learning community, to the mentee, and to the mentor. The learning community benefits by having its values and practices passed on to the incoming faculty. The stability of the community is preserved through mentoring.

The staff member being mentored gains by having help in the difficult first year in the areas of curriculum and instruction, classroom management, administrative requirements, and policies. Teachers often receive social and emotional support from their mentors, as well.

For the mentor, the experience frequently results in increased reflection, heightened zeal, and fresh perspectives about teaching and learning. A long-lasting friendship may be an additional bonus for both the mentor and the protégé.

Tips for Leaders 7.3

Match Making

Matching mentors and mentees works best when

- The mentor is willing.
- They teach comparable students or the same or similar subjects.
- They have a common planning time.
- They both have been provided with orientation to the mentoring process.

Roles and Responsibilities of Mentors

The chief function of a mentor is to help the novice become an independent, highly effective member of the professional learning community. The successful mentor establishes a relationship with the mentee based on trust, confidentiality, and support. In addition to fostering the development of pedagogical skills, the mentor passes on information about procedures and the culture of the learning community. A mentor, at times, serves as a coach, an assessor, and a guide (Portner, 1998). Mentors are often role models, as well. There is much advice in the literature about mentoring. In addition to the many books written for the mentoring teacher, practical information about mentorship is available for the first-year teacher, such as the work of Roberts (2001).

Careful thought must be given to selecting mentors because their role in passing on the culture and standards of the community is so important. Some qualities to look for in a mentor are presented below.

The mentor should

- Be an outstanding teacher with high standards of professionalism.
- Be a learner and value inquiry and reflection.
- Have knowledge of policies, procedures, and pedagogy.
- Be patient, understanding, accessible, helpful, confident, and trustworthy.
- Understand the adult learner (Portner, 1998). Just because someone is an excellent teacher of children does not mean that he or she is able to relate to adults in the same way. (Strategies for working with adult learners are discussed in Chapter 8.)
- Appreciate and understand diversity and its impact on learning in mentees as well as in students (Crow & Matthews, 1998). Differences

in backgrounds in our increasingly pluralistic society may affect perspectives about teaching and learning.

- Be willing and able to invest the necessary time and energy to the mentoring relationship. Sometimes personal or professional obligations might prevent the best teachers from fulfilling mentoring responsibilities effectively.

Principals, assistant principals, supervisors, and other administrators need mentors, too. Often, the new administrator is the sole person in the building in that role and has no one right at hand to turn to for assistance. Informal mentoring sometimes happens among administrators. However, districts should not depend on this and should establish formal mentoring programs for new administrators. Such programs can vitalize leadership and become a source of ongoing professional development for the principals and assistant principals serving as mentors (Crow & Matthews, 1998).

As an example, one of the authors was involved in a mentorship program for 127 new principals. The mentors provided technical and emotional support for the new administrators. The program also established networks and support groups that helped reduce the isolation of the new principals. Although the program focused on the new administrators, the mentors also derived great benefits: They reported an increased sense of job satisfaction and professional growth as a result of their mentoring role.

Strategies for Implementing Mentoring Programs

Here are some strategies you can employ as you implement a mentoring program:

- After selecting the mentors, provide a training program for them (Crow & Matthews, 1998). This should include the procedures to be followed as well as communication skills to help them relate more effectively to the mentees.
- Conduct an orientation program for mentors and their protégés. This session should outline the roles and responsibilities of both participants and allow time for them to meet together in pairs.
- Establish a support group for mentors. Set a time when mentors can get together to discuss emerging problems and share ideas with one another.
- Start a group for new teachers so that the incoming cohorts may get to know one another and provide support to each other as they go through that difficult first year.

- Before beginning the mentoring project, decide on how it will be evaluated. During and after the program, assess and make adjustments as needed. Participants' comments should be part of the evaluation.
- Have an annual meeting for mentors and protégés. It will give basic information to those new to the program and will serve as a reflective vehicle for those returning as mentors.
- Encourage experienced mentors to serve as informal mentors of new mentors.
- Publicize the mentorship program to staff, parents, and students and explain how it supports the learning community (Ganser, 2001). For example, the Evergreen School, mentioned previously, describes its mentorship program on its Website.

Tips for Effective Mentoring

Below are some helpful tips for mentors:

- Establish a friendly and informal relationship with your mentees. Invite them for coffee or lunch and get to know them informally. Have frequent, informal contact with them both in and outside the classroom.
- Support an understanding of diversity (Denmark & Podsen, 2000).
- Get to know your mentee's needs and concerns. You can do this with direct questions or by observing them (Portner, 1998).
- Establish short- and long-term goals together.
- Pass on information about the school, its policies, procedures, and cultures.
- Transmit pedagogical information through discussion, demonstration, observation, and feedback.
- Encourage the mentees to reflect on their practice.
- Know when to let the teacher become independent (Portner, 1998). The ultimate purpose of mentoring is to foster competent professionals who can make their own contributions to the community of learners.

HOW MAY ISSUES OF EQUITY AND DIVERSITY BE ADDRESSED IN A COLLABORATIVE LEARNING COMMUNITY?

Pat Martin is sitting with Mr. Patel and Mrs. Diaz in the faculty room. Pat is concerned about making a connection with one of his students. He says, "He's a nice kid, but whenever I talk to him, he looks away or looks down. I don't know if he's afraid of me or dislikes me or if he's just overly shy. Could it be that he's suffering from low self-esteem or something? I just can't figure it out."

Mrs. Diaz says, "Oh, I know who you mean. It's none of those things, Pat. In that child's home, it is expected that children look down when adults talk to them. It is considered a sign of respect. In fact, it would be considered rude and defiant for a child to look an adult straight in the eye. In the American culture, we value eye contact, but not every culture does. I've seen some of my colleagues get furious about this very thing when they are scolding a youngster and the youngster doesn't look at them. They yell at the child, 'Look at me when I'm talking to you.' They just don't understand." She shakes her head sadly.

"Oh" says Pat. "So he is actually showing me respect when he looks down like that. I'm glad you told me that. I never would have figured that out by myself."

Pat's experience is just a small example of what occurs when educators and students are of different cultures. Misunderstandings may result, some of which have much more serious implications than this illustration. Cultural misunderstandings may cause barriers not only between teachers and students, but among staff members. Worse, lack of understanding may lead to conscious or unconscious stereotyping, misinformation, and even conflict. Curriculum content and materials may be inaccurate or incomplete in terms of the contributions of various groups.

Diversity is an issue that must be addressed if a school is to be changed into a learning community. As Nieto (2002) points out, we must raise concerns about equity and access, even if it is disturbing to do so. We must provide a quality education for all of our students, regardless of their background or gender. Furthermore, this education must enable them to live in the real world, in which people of many different cultures increasingly come in contact with one another.

This also means that the staff members will be more diverse. Collaboration in learning communities means that people will increasingly be working closely with others who are very different from themselves. Questions such as those in Tips for Leaders 7.4 help to break down barriers between teachers so that they may collaborate more harmoniously. A collaborative approach in addressing diversity and equity is beneficial because staff members can help one another expand their insights and understandings. Pat was fortunate that his team is quite diverse and that Mrs. Diaz understood the

Tips for Leaders 7.4

Looking at Our Cultures

An approach to looking at diversity that we have found successful is conducting a series of discussions on various aspects of culture. In small groups, people discuss topics such as those listed below. The small groups then share their ideas with the large group. In the large group discussion, we talk about the examples and the underlying values they represent. These sessions help participants to become more aware of their own beliefs and practices on a conscious level. In addition, they find out more about their colleagues and gain a greater understanding of them. It is beneficial to make the small groups as diverse as possible in order to get a variety of perspectives.

Here are some possible discussion topics:

- What was your family's approach to child rearing when you were a child?
- What was your family's belief about healing and health issues?
- What are some of your traditions around marriage and weddings?

cultural background of his student and explained it to him. The learning community cannot rely solely on informal approaches to diversity and equity; a concerted effort should be put forth to address these issues. Following are some basic strategies for weaving equity and appreciation of diversity into the fabric of the learning community that we have found effective.

Strategies for Collaboratively Addressing Equity and Diversity

Work to Break Down Barriers Between Staff Members

As previously mentioned, staff members of diverse backgrounds are expected to work collaboratively in the learning community. Barriers between diverse staff members must be overcome so that they may work together more effectively. Our experience has been that small group discussions in a nonthreatening atmosphere and planned approaches such as the following facilitate the process.

Tips for Leaders 7.5

Examining Our Own Educational Beliefs

In a staff development session, allow time for teachers to reflect on and discuss in dyads or triads the questions below. Once the conversation gets going, more topics will emerge.

- What were your family's views and feelings on school and learning? Recall some things they did that demonstrated these views.
- What was the outlook toward school and learning in your community?
- What do you believe about education and learning?
- What are your thoughts about [Asians, Blacks, Hispanics, girls, boys, poor children, rich children, handicapped children] in school and the way they learn?
- What are your thoughts about immigrants?

Provide Opportunities for Teachers to Examine Their Own Cultures

Teachers need to look at their own cultures and how they affect their beliefs and worldviews. It is often hard to examine our own culture; we take it so for granted (Trumbell, Rothstein-Fisch, & Greenfield, 2001). Reflective questions and structured activities are good starting points.

Examine Beliefs and Assumptions About Education

The staff members need to examine their beliefs about education, their assumptions about learning, and their ways of teaching in conjunction with the diverse population groups with whom they work. More specifically, they need to understand how their backgrounds affect what and how they expect children to learn. Teachers may have unconscious assumptions about students who come from different backgrounds in relation to their schooling. Once aware of them, teachers can begin to change their practices.

Promote Opportunities for Staff to Learn About Other Cultures

The staff should understand the cultures of others, particularly of the students with whom they are working and of the others on their teams. It

Tips for Leaders 7.6

Examining the Learning Community in Terms of Equity and Diversity

The following questions may be used to get staff members to look at issues of diversity and equity in the learning community. Encourage staff members to develop their own questions as well.

- Do the images in the classrooms reflect this country's diversity in terms of race, culture, age, and/or physical ability?
- Do the library, audiovisual, and other materials reflect this diversity?
- Are they free of stereotypes?
- Does the curriculum recognize the contributions of all segments of the population?
- Are members of our staff given equal opportunities regardless of gender, race, ethnicity, religion, or physical handicaps?

is not enough to be aware of the top layer of culture, such as music, food, and holidays. It is important to try to learn about the deeper layers of culture that have to do with beliefs, values, and worldviews.

An approach that we have found successful is to have people of different ethnic background discuss their personal experiences with bias in school settings. The most memorable example for us of this approach was a session involving a diverse group of students from the high school who talked to an elementary school faculty. Teachers gained great insights through this dialogue that would have been hard to get otherwise. It was a powerful session.

Develop Questions/Guidelines

Develop questions/guidelines for ensuring equity and respecting diversity in the learning community. Using the information gained from the above activities, staff members should develop questions they ask themselves to ensure equity and a respect for diversity as they work with one another, develop curriculum, assess student work, and engage in other aspects of the educational program. In the school of one of the authors, the staff collaborated in developing an antibias questionnaire to be used by staff for self evaluation. The process of developing it was as helpful in examining bias as the questionnaire itself.

Tips for Leaders 7.7

Improving Cultural Relationships in the Learning Community

- Provide diversity training for the staff, students, and parents.
- Handle incidents of bias or discrimination promptly.
- Make concerted efforts to involve parents and students of all backgrounds in the life of the school.
- Incorporate diversity and equity into all areas of the curriculum.
- Learn as much as possible about the cultures of the students you serve.
- Sponsor events that celebrate diversity, such as international dinners or multicultural performances.
- Use nonbiased language.
- Use objective data to keep an eye on issues of equity and make corrections as necessary.

Collaborative Examination

Collaboratively examine the texts, other instructional materials, and school policies and practices. Parents and community may be helpful collaborators in this process. Errors of omission or commission regarding issues of diversity and equity must be identified and corrected. For example, a school district in which one of the authors worked reserved the right to reject texts and materials found to be racist or sexist. This policy was stamped on every purchase order. A committee, which included parents and community members, examined all texts for bias.

Maintain the Effort

It is important that the activities mentioned above be ongoing. As the student body or the staff demographics change, there is a need to renew the efforts. As circumstances within and between groups evolve, more study will become necessary. Elliot and Schiff (2001) point out that staff development should include ongoing inquiry and reflection about issues surrounding equity.

Staff members must constantly examine their own attitudes about race, class, gender, and ethnicity to ensure that stereotypical beliefs do not creep in to disrupt their collegial relationships, interfere with the success of all students, or negatively impact any aspect of the learning community.

Information Online 7.2

More information about parent involvement may be found at the Website of the National PTA, http://pta.org/parentinvolvement/standards/pfisand.asp.

HOW MAY WE COLLABORATE WITH PARENTS IN LEARNING COMMUNITIES?

Parents are partners in the learning community, and both students and schools benefit from their involvement. Family involvement is linked to student achievement at all grade levels: The more involved parents and families are, the better the student performance. Families know the youngsters in ways that teachers do not and so can add a different perspective. Furthermore, families who are involved in the learning community tend to support it in many ways. They can, for example, be advocates for the school in helping to pass budgets and promoting school improvement.

National standards for parental involvement identify six major categories in which learning communities and families may collaborate. These are communicating, parenting, student learning, volunteering, decision making, and collaborating with the community (National PTA, 2001–2002).[1] Some strategies we have found effective in these areas are shared below.

Home-School Communication

- Call every parent toward the beginning of the year with something positive about his or her child. One of the writers, as a principal, encouraged her teachers to do this and found that those who did had far fewer problems with parents. It establishes a relationship so that, if a call about a problem is necessary later on, it's much easier to deal with.
- Establish two-way communication systems, such as e-mail and voice mail, that parents can access at all hours.
- Hold some conferences and meetings at times convenient for parents who are not available during the day. As a principal, one of the authors held early morning breakfast meetings for parents who could not attend at other times.
- Translate notices into other languages, when possible, for parents who do not read English.

Parenting

- Conduct workshops on parenting skills. Guest speakers may sometimes be found among the parent body. We have had pediatricians, psychologists, and nurses among the parents who have run workshops for other parents.
- Provide transportation to these workshops for parents who need it through car pools or school bus if transportation is a problem in your area.
- Offer childcare during the parent workshops. We have found that attendance improves when babysitting is available.
- Connect parents to family support services in the community as the need arises.

Student Learning

- Advise parents of the academic expectations for each grade.
- Recommend books and activities that will reinforce learning. Although we did this throughout the year, parents found suggestions for summer reading and activities particularly helpful.
- At times, give homework that involves parents and children working together.
- Plan workshops for parents on aspects of the curriculum. Some of our most popular evenings were hands-on workshops in which the parents experienced learning in the same way as their children.
- Hold family nights where parents and children can experience learning together and have fun, too. Many schools sponsor family math nights or family science nights, which involve hands-on activities for families working in groups.

Volunteering

- Use family members as tutors, translators, and classroom volunteers.
- Encourage family members to share their talents, hobbies, or aspects of their culture in the classrooms to enrich and extend the curriculum.
- Allow parents to lead special events, such as school fairs and school beautification projects. A parent in a school where one of the authors was principal chaired Earth Day activities for the school. In later years, she ended up doing it for the whole town.
- Organize parents to coordinate the cultural arts programs. In some of the schools where one of the authors was principal, the parents arranged the arts assemblies for the year with input from the principal. They attended the showcases to select artists and took care of contacting the performers for assemblies and artists-in-residence programs.

- Have parents conduct tours of the school for new and prospective parents and distribute school information packets. Our experience has been that the parent-to-parent contact complements the welcome from the principal and helps new parents feel part of the community.

Decision Making

- Include parents on school and district advisory boards and committees.
- Make a special effort to reach out to segments of the population that are usually not represented in such activities.
- Get input from parents when changing such items as report cards, grading systems, and promotion requirements. When we involved parents as were designing new report cards, the end result was much more useful to them.
- Involve parents in defining the school vision and in formulating policies and procedures that affect their children.

Collaborating With the Community

- Involve parents in seeking resources and services for the school from businesses and institutions in the community.
- Have parents participate in setting up community service experiences for students.

Collaborating with parents in these six areas enhances the bonds between those most interested in the students, their families, and their teachers and helps to make the learning community stronger.

CONCLUSION

Collaboration is the glue that keeps learning communities together. A wide variety of collaborative approaches are used for the improvement of instruction, including looking at student work together and mentoring. Diversity, with the many perspectives it affords, brings greater effectiveness to collaboration. Thought must be given to issues of equity and diversity in all aspects of collaboration. The importance of parents as partners in the learning community should never be minimized. Parents can play a wide variety of roles in supporting and enriching their children's education. Through collaboration, parents and educators of diverse backgrounds can find many ways to work together in the learning community to enhance the educational process and achieve improved outcomes for all students.

ACTIVITIES

1. Take a careful look at your classroom—the images on the walls or bulletin boards, the audio-visual materials, the books in the classroom library, and the other materials in the room. Do they reflect the diversity in your class and the country at large? Do they support equity? Reflect and research how you can make your learning environment more representative of diversity and supportive of equity.

2. Think of someone who served as a mentor to you. What were the personal and professional qualities that made this a successful relationship? What would have made it better?

3. Research and discuss with colleagues the various protocols and procedures for looking at student work.

4. Develop a program of collaboration with families in your school using the six categories identified by National PTA for parental involvement. Involve parents in designing the program.

NOTE

1. Excerpted with permission from National PTA's National Standards for Parent/Family Involvement Programs. Copyright © 1998.

8 Learning Through Professional Portfolios

PREVIEW OF THE CHAPTER

Ongoing and vigorous learning on the part of the teachers is an essential element of professional learning communities. It is important that the faculty members continuously examine their own growth and development and reflect on their practice. The professional portfolio is a powerful tool for facilitating this process. This chapter discusses professional portfolios in the learning community and offers strategies for their development. Among the questions it seeks to answer are the following:

- What is a professional portfolio?
- What is the role of professional portfolios in the learning community?
- What goes into a professional portfolio?
- How do you get started developing the portfolio?
- How should the portfolio be organized?
- What about electronic portfolios?
- How may the portfolio be evaluated?
- What strategies support the use of portfolios in the learning community?

WHAT IS A PROFESSIONAL PORTFOLIO?

The teachers in the faculty room in a school in the Menlo School District are discussing their students' portfolios. "The kids seem to get a kick out of looking through their portfolios periodically. They enjoy seeing actual evidence of their growth," says Ms. Gold. "Yes," agrees Mr. Molloy. "You know, it might be a good idea for us to keep a portfolio of our work as well."

"I had to do that when I was in school," excitedly interjected Ms. Wing, a new teacher.

"What? Were you an art major?" asks Ms. Gold.

"No, it was part of our field experience course. We had to collect samples of our work, and student work, and write reflections about what we had learned."

"Well, I've kept a collection of student work, letters from parents and administrators, articles I wrote, and photographs for years. In fact, I have several huge scrapbooks now," says Ms. Gold. "I guess that I've been keeping a portfolio without realizing it."

"No, that's not really a portfolio," Ms. Wing replies. "What you could do to create a portfolio from those things you have collected is select a few items that you feel express your philosophy or that represent important benchmarks in your professional development. Then, you need to write reflections on the significance of these items in your practice. It's a great way to document and examine your own growth and change over the years."

"Yes, that's more like what I had in mind when I talked about teachers keeping portfolios. In addition to making us examine our practice, I think it would help us in working with the youngsters with their portfolios," says Mr. Molloy.

"Why don't we all start professional portfolios and help one another through the process?" ventures Ms. Gold.

"That's how we did it in our courses," blurts out Ms. Wing enthusiastically. "We each made our own portfolio, but we worked in small groups and showed them to one another and talked about them. Some of the questions my classmates asked me during our discussions really helped me to focus on why I was doing what I was doing and helped me to clarify and articulate my approach to teaching. It was a great experience, and I would welcome a continuation of it now that I am in my own classroom."

The three teachers decide to work on professional portfolios together. As we leave them, they are planning the details of their newest collaborative learning experience.

A professional portfolio is a thoughtful document demonstrating a teacher's approach to teaching or an administrator's approach to leadership. It offers a portrait of the educator's practice over time and reflections about it (Martin-Kniep, 1999). Documents chosen for the portfolio reflect key points of an educator's philosophy and professional growth. They provide evidence to support the reflections on philosophy and practice that the educator writes for the portfolio. The portfolio is a living reflection of a teacher's career and inner professional life. In the learning community, collegial inquiry, research, and reflection guide the development and review of the professional portfolio.

Portfolios often take book form. However, with the growth of technology, many teachers now create computer-based presentations and even put their portfolios on a Website on the Internet. No matter what form portfolios take, they offer selected evidence of practice accompanied by carefully considered reflections.

Frequently, people keep two kinds of portfolios. One is a working portfolio and the other is a presentation, or showcase, portfolio (Campbell, Cignetti, Melenyzer, Nettles, Wyman, 2001). These are described below.

The working portfolio contains complete collections of evidence: for example, detailed units, extensive photographs of classroom activities, and many samples of student work. In addition, work in progress is kept in the working portfolio. Reflective comments are also included. This is a dynamic, ever-changing document.

The presentation or showcase portfolio is smaller and more focused than the working portfolio. Items for the showcase portfolio are chosen from the working portfolio. It might include a few sample photographs or one video of classroom activities instead of the whole collection, a summary of a unit rather than the entire unit, or one example of teacher-made material as opposed to the complete set. The showcase portfolio should be easy for the viewer to handle and understand. It should be well organized, streamlined, and attractive, and should give viewers a quick overview of the author's professional practice and philosophy. The showcase portfolio should be tailored for its purpose and audience.

Self-assessment and reflection are the most important functions of a portfolio in terms of an educator's professional growth (Bullock and Hawk, 2001). All types of portfolios have this aspect in common, but a self-assessment portfolio is done by the teacher for him- or herself. It should be an ongoing project, and it will change from year to year as the teacher has new experiences and gains new insights. The teacher determines what goes in it based on his or her own criteria, but in a learning community will discuss the selections with colleagues. Whether done alone or collaboratively, serious consideration to the portfolio helps teachers in reflecting on their practice in relation to their beliefs. It may cause them to reconsider or even change some practices, or it may lead them to new understandings.

WHAT IS THE ROLE OF PROFESSIONAL PORTFOLIOS IN THE LEARNING COMMUNITY?

For some years, there has been interest in portfolios for students as an alternative way of assessing and documenting their progress. More recently, attention has been given to professional portfolios for teachers. There are many purposes for developing a portfolio, and these change at various points in one's professional career. Portfolios help prospective new teachers support and document their learning. Often, these portfolios are developed and discussed with classmates. In the opening vignette, Ms. Wing referred to this type of portfolio. Preservice portfolios may be used during the employment interview. As pointed out by Irby and Brown (2000), professional portfolios give candidates an edge in employment interviews. Many teachers take their preservice portfolios into their classrooms and continue to develop them. The use of professional portfolios has spread to experienced teachers, too, as depicted in the Menlo School scenario. In some school systems, professional portfolios may be used in lieu of the usual annual evaluation. Sometimes, a portfolio is helpful for documenting professional accomplishments, effective instructional strategies, or classroom research in order to qualify for promotions or compete for special bonuses, awards, or grants (Wolf, 1996). Administrators keep portfolios for many of the same reasons as teachers. Reflection on the part of administrators is important for maintaining a healthy learning community (Martin-Kniep, 1999).

The movement toward the use of professional portfolios by experienced educators has been given impetus by national and state programs. For example, the National Boards for Professional Teaching Standards emphasize a professional model of assessment whereby teachers document their own competence rather than having someone else evaluate them. Similarly, standards of the Interstate New Teacher Assessment and Support Consortium (INTASC) call for new teachers to substantiate their proficiency by means of a portfolio (Bullock & Hawk, 2001).

Professional portfolios offer benefits to the educator involved, to the students, and to the learning community in general. The primary gain for

---

Tips for Leaders 8.1

Inform Them

If professional portfolios are required or optional for yearly evaluation, increment, or promotion, be sure that the teachers understand the requirements and criteria well before they begin developing the portfolio.

---

educators in maintaining a portfolio is the opportunity to reflect on and document their professional practices in relation to their beliefs (Irby & Brown, 2000). It helps them to trace their career growth and make plans for the future. Keeping a professional portfolio can encourage teachers and administrators to engage in research and question their practice. The underlying aim of professional portfolios is to improve practice so that the students get the best quality education possible.

Ideally, students benefit from the use of professional portfolios through improved instruction. Results with students should be an important part of the portfolio. This provides evidence of the direct connection between teaching and learning. As teachers document their practice and reflect on their effectiveness, or lack thereof, they make adjustments to upgrade their professional competencies. The ultimate purpose of the professional portfolio is to inform instruction and increase student learning.

Students benefit in another way when their teachers maintain their own portfolios. Going through the process themselves gives teachers a better understanding of the nuances of decision making and the skills and problems involved in putting together a portfolio. It enables teachers to work more successfully with students on student portfolios (Painter, 2001).

A benefit to the learning community and to education in general is that a portfolio provides a vehicle for preserving samples of outstanding teaching or leadership (Wolf, 1996). All too often, a highly successful lesson or leadership approach goes undocumented. Recording and documenting it in a professional portfolio conserves it for future consideration and maybe even for publication.

The learning community is enhanced when educators keep professional portfolios, especially when they work on them collegially. Collaborative development and review of professional portfolios is a very powerful tool for professional growth and helps in building a learning community. Some teachers and administrators say that using portfolios helped them collaborate to improve instruction and student outcomes (Van Wagenen & Hibbard, 1998). Professional portfolios encourage reflection and research on the part of educators. This is multiplied when colleagues develop their portfolios together or review one another's portfolios. Collaborative portfolio development helps to diminish the isolation of educators as they share their portfolios, discuss their practice, and exchange ideas about teaching and learning. Teachers often report that their collaborative portfolio experiences give them a greater sense of community. This is likely to happen to the teachers in the Menlo School as well.

WHAT GOES INTO A PROFESSIONAL PORTFOLIO?

Evidence and reflections are the two major elements in a portfolio. The next two sections will address these. However, Bullock and Hawk (2001) offer a word of caution to teachers as they select their evidence and write their reflections: Be aware of issues of legality and privacy, especially if the portfolio will be viewed outside of the school. Avoid revealing students' identities in work samples or reflections. Find out what the policies of the school and district are in regard to permissions and release forms.

Evidence

Evidence provides the actual documentation of practice. The selection of evidence should, in addition to considering the purpose of and potential audience for the portfolio as a whole, reflect the aspects of professionalism the author wishes to emphasize, such as teacher/administrator as curriculum developer, as researcher, or as a designer of professional development (Martin-Kniep, 1999). In collaborative development of the portfolio, teachers discuss with colleagues their reasons for these selections. Often, a remark or a question from colleagues will help the teacher to more clearly understand and articulate the significance of a document. Some items that might be included in the portfolio are listed below.

- A statement of your teaching philosophy.
- Discussion of your approach to teaching and learning and the context in which it occurs.
- A description of how you identify student strengths and needs and how you meet them.
- Samples of lessons, units, or strategies.

- Examples of student work—individual or group projects.
- Documentation of student achievement.
- Articles or other professional publications you have written.
- Results of classroom research you conducted.
- Documentation of conferences, study groups, or workshops you have led or of consultancies.
- Work done in professional associations on the school, local, state, or national level.
- Steps you have taken to improve your teaching practice.
- The impact that professional books, journal articles, or educational research has had on your practice.

Reflective Commentary

In addition to these documents, it is important to include some written thoughts on what the document represents in relation to your philosophy or practice and what you have learned as a professional. Reflection on practice and beliefs is what separates professional portfolios from collections in scrapbooks (Bullock & Hawk, 2001). It is through reflection that the educator gains illumination about his or her own practice and that the viewer obtains an understanding of the author as an educator. Reflections provide an individual portrait of the teacher as a life-long learner. The reflection should include a description of the context of the evidence and should openly discuss positive or negative aspects of the evidence. Authors should explain how it has impacted them and how it will affect their future planning. The implications for future practice are perhaps the most important part of the reflection, for this is where the learning is articulated (Irby & Brown, 2000). In the learning community, collaborative reflection about the documents encourages conversations and insights about the instructional process. Such dialogue helps to further strengthen the community.

Some other tips for portfolio reflections include the following:

- Be personal. Express your own ideas and feelings, and write in the first-person rather than in the impersonal third-person voice.
- Be viewer-friendly, especially if you are writing for an audience other than yourself. Be sure that content and language are appropriate for your audience and purpose. Express your thoughts clearly and in an organized manner.
- Be sensitive. Use acceptable terms, especially when referring to ethnic groups or special needs students. Avoid slang, stereotypes, or outmoded usage. Be careful when referring to individual students or colleagues (Bullock & Hawk, 2001).

Figure 8.1   Prompt Questions for Discussing a Portfolio Lesson

- Why did you teach this specific lesson?
- Why did you choose to teach it in this way?
- What did you like about the lesson?
- What would you have done differently?
- Did you accomplish your goals?
- What did the students learn?
- How do you know that they learned?
- What did you learn as a result of this lesson?
- How will this knowledge impact on your practice?
- Why are you including this lesson in your portfolio?

- Be analytical. Consider the meaning of the document to you, why you chose it, and what you learned as a result of it (Irby & Brown, 2000).
- Share your personal reflections with your colleagues. Be open to their comments. Engage in dialogue with colleagues about their reflections. See Figure 8.1 for examples of questions for discussing a lesson included in the portfolio.

HOW DO YOU GET STARTED DEVELOPING A PORTFOLIO?

There is no one way to develop a portfolio. The way one goes about it varies according to the purpose and the personality of the teacher involved. Teachers who work on their portfolios together may decide collaboratively on the format and the process. The literature offers extensive guidance for educators preparing their portfolios. See, for example, Bullock and Hawk (2001), Campbell et al. (2001), and Wyatt and Looper (1999). Here are a few suggestions from them and from our own knowledge base to get you started. All of these activities may be done cooperatively with your colleagues in the learning community.

- Choose appropriate containers for the working portfolio. Boxes, file drawers, folders, and notebooks all may help to keep your artifacts organized.
- Define the purpose and audience for the portfolio.
- Decide on the format. Will it be in the form of a book? A computer-based presentation? A video? A Website?

- Reflect on your educational beliefs and your professional practice in relation to these beliefs before drafting your outline.
- Think about what types of artifacts or evidence will document these beliefs and where you will get them.
- Collect sample artifacts that relate to these beliefs and to the purpose of the portfolio.
- Date all items and make notes about them as soon as you collect them.
- From this collection, select documents or artifacts that are of high quality and understandable to the viewer, especially for a presentation folder.
- If the portfolio has to meet an outside viewer's criteria, such as for an evaluation, be sure all items are in accordance.

HOW SHOULD THE PORTFOLIO BE ORGANIZED?

There is no one way to organize a portfolio. It is important that your materials be arranged in an attractive, logical way, whether it is in book or electronic format. Figures 8.2 and 8.3 show sample Tables of Contents. Other things to consider as you organize your portfolio include the following:

- If the portfolio is for yourself, you may wish to arrange it around your various roles as a teacher or administrator, such as planning, curriculum development, research, or assessment.
- If the portfolio is being done in conjunction with colleagues, you may prefer to jointly decide on its format and organization.
- If it is for an external reviewer, arrange it according to their criteria.
- It should have a table of contents.
- Start with an introductory statement.
- Be sure that every item presented in the portfolio has a rationale.
- Articulate the rationale to your colleagues. Doing so helps teachers to clarify their thoughts and also helps in creating a community of learners.
- Before submitting a presentation portfolio in any form, view it in its entirety to be sure that it gives an accurate picture of you as an educator and that the evidence supports your statements.

WHAT ABOUT ELECTRONIC PORTFOLIOS?

Electronic portfolios are gaining in popularity. As Powers, Thompson, and Buckner (2001) point out, they have about the same information that is in a traditional portfolio, but they are developed and accessed electronically. Videos, scanned material, digital photographs, text, and audio are included in this format. The same basic guidelines for traditional portfolios in terms of

Figure 8.2   Sample Teaching Portfolio Table of Contents

Table of Contents

1. Introduction
2. My Teaching Philosophy
3. Examples of Student Cooperative Projects
4. Examples of Lesson Plans
5. Student Reactions and Achievements
6. Parent/Family Involvement
7. Workshops I Have Presented

purpose and content apply to electronic portfolios, but there are additional considerations having to do with technology.

On the positive side, electronic portfolios offer more variety both for the viewer and for the developer, and they have the added value of being interactive. Vast amounts of material may be stored in them and they are easily transportable. An electronic portfolio may be viewed by many people in spread out locations simultaneously.

However, creating an electronic portfolio requires a certain level of sophistication in technological skills and access to hardware and software, which the author may not have. Some potential viewers may not have the computer platform that is compatible to your portfolio, or their equipment may not be able to support a multimedia presentation.

The three primary ways of developing electronic portfolios are with portfolio design software, multimedia authoring software, and Web page design software (Powers et al., 2001). The choice depends on the material to be included, the proposed audiences for the portfolio, and the technological skills of the developer. Some tips for developing electronic portfolios compiled from Irby and Brown (2000) and Powers et al. (2001) and our own experiences are offered below.

- Be sure that your electronic portfolio looks professional. If you do not have the technical skills, get some one who does to develop it.
- Choose a format that is accessible to your anticipated viewers and compatible with their hardware.
- Make certain that the mechanics, such as the links, are working.
- Pay attention to the content of your electronic portfolio. Avoid getting so caught up in the technology that you forget about the quality of the content.
- Make your electronic portfolio easy to use and easy to maintain.

Figure 8.3   Sample Administrator's Portfolio Table of Contents

Table of Contents

1. Educational Philosophy/Vision Statement
2. Setting and Role Description
3. Challenges/Research Questions
4. Goals and Objectives
5. Strategies
6. Accomplishments

- Be cautious about the personal information you put on a Web-based portfolio for security reasons.
- Make both a hard copy and a backup electronic copy of your portfolio.
- Have your colleagues view your electronic portfolio, make comments, and raise questions. Collaboration around electronic portfolios is as important as around traditional ones.

One of the writers helps graduate students in the administration courses to design their own electronic portfolios, and they are very enthusiastic about the process. One student said that, although he was initially opposed to the idea of creating an electronic portfolio, he came to realize that it is easier to keep than a traditional one. He added that he enjoyed the experience and that it got him more involved with Web pages in general. As technology expands and more educators achieve technical sophistication, it is very likely that electronic portfolios will surpass traditional ones in a few years. Perhaps the teachers in Menlo will do theirs electronically as well.

HOW MAY THE PORTFOLIO BE EVALUATED?

Assessment of the portfolio depends on the purpose for which it was developed. For example, if it was developed as part of, or in lieu of, the yearly evaluation it will be assessed against the criteria established by the school or district for this purpose. If it is for National Board Certification, then those standards will be used. There are several types of rubrics for assessing different types of portfolios (Martin-Kniep, 1999). In the learning community, assessment of professional portfolios may be done jointly. Collaborative assessment of professional portfolios continues the conversations among colleagues about teaching and learning and can be an important tool for professional growth. Collay et al. (1998) suggest that portfolio assessment, as well as development, is best done in groups and that these groups should be formed early in the school year. In general, anyone looking at the portfolio, including the developer, may ask questions like these:

- Are the documents or artifacts presented relevant to the purpose of the portfolio? (Campbell et al., 2001)
- Does the evidence support the claims that are being made? (Bullock & Hawk, 2001)
- Does it demonstrate serious reflection, self-assessment, inquiry, and new insights on the part of the teacher? (Van Wagenen & Hibbard, 1998)
- Does it examine student achievement or student reaction?
- Is the portfolio logically arranged and neatly presented?
- Is it easily accessible and understandable to the viewer?
- Does it present evidence of professional growth and ongoing learning? (Van Wagenen & Hibbard, 1998)

WHAT STRATEGIES SUPPORT THE USE OF PORTFOLIOS IN THE LEARNING COMMUNITY?

Providing time, resources, and moral support can strengthen the use of portfolios in the learning community, as discussed below.

Developing professional portfolios is time-consuming work. Administrators should ensure sufficient uninterrupted time on a regular basis for teachers to get together to work on and review their portfolios. This is especially important when the development and review of professional portfolios is used as a strategy for professional development and building a community of learners.

Making the necessary material and equipment available encourages portfolio development. Supplying file boxes, folders, notebooks, binders, and pages for traditional portfolios and making electronic software and hardware accessible makes it easier for teachers to work on their portfolios. In addition to supplying materials, leaders should recognize that teachers new to the process may need extra support and should assign mentors to those developing portfolios for the first time.

If teachers are doing their portfolios electronically, they should be given the technical assistance they need, whether it be help from the computer teacher in creating a Website or a good software program that supports professional portfolios.

A supportive attitude on the part of administrators, one that recognizes and values the use of portfolios in the learning community is also imperative. It is very important for the administrators to maintain professional portfolios themselves. Just as teachers who keep portfolios are better able to work with students on their own portfolios, so administrators who maintain portfolios are better able to lead their staff in this particular aspect of ongoing learning.

The skill of reflection is vital to portfolio development. Leaders can foster greater reflection by giving teachers reflective prompts in other professional development experiences (Martin-Kniep, 1999). For example, in a workshop on classroom management, teachers might be asked to reflect on such questions as, *What is my greatest classroom management challenge? What strategies have I used to address them? To what degree have they worked? How do I know?* Encouraging journal writing helps teachers to be reflective and gets them in the habit of writing their thoughts.

CONCLUSION

Professional portfolios are an important element in the learning community. Their development supports ongoing learning on the part of the staff, as they document and examine their own instructional approaches. Portfolios can take many forms and may be in traditional or electronic format. Their use encourages teachers to reflect on their practices and their beliefs and ultimately to improve instruction. Collaborative development and review of professional portfolios is a powerful tool for staff development. Engaging in conversation with colleagues about actual practice and sharing insights gained from their protfolios is a valuable process that can help transform a faculty into a community of learners. It is a valuable process that can help transform a faculty into a community of learners.

ACTIVITIES

1. Write out your educational philosophy or beliefs. Using this as a guide, prepare a professional portfolio for yourself. Be sure to write a reflective piece about each artifact or document you select for inclusion. Have a colleague review your portfolio to see whether the documents you have selected support your initial statements and to review the portfolio in general. Engage in conversations about the evidence and the reflective comments in the portfolio.

2. Review your colleague's portfolio in the same way. Exchange ideas about teaching and learning based on insights and questions arising from the portfolios.

3. Together, discuss the process of developing and reviewing the portfolio. What insights did you gain as a result of the experience? What questions were raised? How would you change the process? What changes, if any, would you make in the portfolios?

9 Sustaining the Professional Learning Community

PREVIEW OF THE CHAPTER

Sustaining the professional learning community is the ultimate challenge for school reformers. It is not enough to establish a professional learning community; measures have to be put in place to ensure that the learning community maintains itself. In schools, it must be remembered that the process of change takes place over time (Hall & Hord, 2001). Additionally, the context of teaching is constantly changing, making it necessary to reexamine our assumptions, our beliefs, and our teaching practices. Presently, shifting demographics and varying societal demands are causing our schools to look for new ways of doing things. New knowledge about teaching and learning and externally imposed mandates require that they revisit their instructional practices, develop new assessment procedures as well as change other aspects of the schooling process. Ideas and practices that were enthusiastically agreed upon when a school began its transformation to a learning community, no matter how carefully designed, need to be revisited in the face of these ongoing environmental shifts.

Leaders cannot wait until the learning community is established to think about sustaining it. The fundamental question that must be addressed from the very beginning is this: *What elements must firmly be in place to motivate and encourage teachers to continually engage in learning activities and act on what they have learned for the benefit of students?* This chapter examines ways of sustaining the shared commitment and focus that is characteristic of learning community schools by addressing the following questions:

- How do we sustain a culture that supports a collaborative approach to improving instructional practice and student outcomes?
- How do we sustain the structures that support learning community schools?
- What must we do to maintain the focus on continuous student learning that characterizes learning communities?
- How do we maintain a focus on the school's mission and shared vision statements that stress student achievement?
- What steps must be taken to ensure that shared leadership is sustained in learning community schools?

It should be noted that all of the strategies described in this chapter are interrelated and mutually reinforcing even though we discuss them separately.

HOW DO WE SUSTAIN A CULTURE THAT SUPPORTS A COLLABORATIVE APPROACH TO IMPROVING INSTRUCTIONAL PRACTICE AND STUDENT OUTCOMES?

School culture is frequently overlooked, but it is one of the most important elements of school life. "Culture is the way things are done." (McEwan, 1998, p. 57). It is an amalgamation of the values, beliefs, and practices of the teachers, staff, and students. It is created through their relationships and experiences, and is reinforced in the traditions, rituals, and ceremonies. This section will examine the culture of the learning community and will discuss the role of celebration and collaboration in sustaining the culture.

Culture of the Learning Community

Culture binds people together. It influences how people behave, what they think, and how they feel in a school (Peterson & Deal, 1998). As discussed in earlier chapters, the culture in a learning community school is student-focused and collaborative. Members share the belief that everyone is a learner. Teachers engage in research and problem solving, examining their practice with the ultimate aim of improving student performance. In

---

Tips for Leaders 9.1

Pass It on

In order to maintain a strong, positive culture in the learning community, it is important to see that the culture is passed on to new teachers. One way is to assign mentors or "buddies" who have good understanding of the school's values and beliefs and who are themselves exemplary to guide these new teachers, model appropriate behaviors, and articulate the underlying beliefs of the school.

---

this culture, collaboration and collegiality are highly valued. Staff members work together, help one another, and share ideas.

Layers of Culture

As Williams and De Gaetano (1985) explain, there are three major layers of culture. Each of these layers is described below. In the deepest layer reside the values, the shared beliefs of the community members. This layer is often so taken for granted that it is difficult for an outsider to see it readily and, indeed, it may be hard for some of the members to articulate at this level. This level represents the "why": *Why do we do things the way we do them?* In some schools, as staff members go through school improvement, they articulate their values in the process of defining the vision and developing a mission statement. This process helps to shed light on that deepest layer. Posting the mission and vision helps to keep them in the conscious mind of community members.

In the middle layer are the activities, the day-to-day practices that make up the ongoing life of the school. This is the "how" layer: *How do we do things around here? How are staff meetings conducted? How are end-of-term transition activities for students conducted? How are parents received into the building?* This layer is more readily visible to the watchful observer than the deepest layer.

On the surface layer are objects, the things that are evident even in the absence of any community members. This is the "what" layer: *What do we see and hear when we walk around the school after hours?* The hall displays, the amount of student work exhibited, the way furniture is arranged, and the slogans that are posted are some of the things that give us clues about

---

Tips for Leaders 9.2

Learn the Layers

It is very important for leaders to understand all the layers of cultures in their school. They need to know the rituals, ceremonies, traditions, and practices. Leaders also need to know and understand the deep values that are behind them. A leader should not try to change a culture without first understanding it and its many layers.

---

the culture of the school. In a community of learners, a focus on student achievement, collaboration, inquiry, problem solving, and continuous improvement should permeate all layers of culture.

Symbols and Rituals

Symbols and rituals are very important in the culture of an organization. They serve to reinforce the values and bond the members together (Peterson & Deal, 1998). Rituals sometimes mark certain benchmarks and accomplishments. In schools, the graduation ceremony is the ultimate ritual. It is one in which the students, staff, parents, families, and the community at large participate. It marks the successful completion of the educational process. It is a ritual full of symbolism, with the cap and robes of the students, the various colors of the hoods and robes of the staff, and the turning of the tassel when the diploma is conferred. However, it is not enough to have rituals and symbols just at the end of the educational process. They are needed throughout the years to become part of the traditions; to reinforce shared values, to motivate the members, and to keep the vision in mind. Symbols and rituals should be part of celebrations.

Stories and Legends

Stories of important people and events in the school serve to inspire members of the learning community and help to reinforce the culture (Noe, 2002). These stories represent the shared values of the community, and the people in the stories serve as role models. Glickman (2003) points out that stories serve to reinforce a school's identity and strengthen the community's commitment to its work. Legends should also be part of celebrations. All of these rituals, symbols, and stories help to sustain the culture of the learning community.

Tips for Leaders 9.3

Symbols, Rituals, and Ceremonies

When celebrating success, incorporate symbols and use rituals in ceremonies that are part of the school's traditions and that are appropriate to the values being extolled. This reinforces the culture and adds to the richness of life in the school.

Celebrations and School Culture

When Pat Martin walks into the faculty meeting in a Menlo School, he immediately sees that something special is about to occur. The room is decorated with balloons and the refreshments are fancier than usual. When the principal comes in, he announces that today is a day of celebration. He goes on to say that student data have been examined and that many of the teams have met or surpassed their goals. He gives awards to teams that have reached their goals. In addition, awards are given to teachers who have performed in outstanding ways to achieve the vision of the school. Recipients include staff developers who came in voluntarily on Saturday mornings to run a tutoring program and the teachers who designed and implemented an orientation program that helped students who came in midyear to adjust socially and academically. In addition to giving individual and team awards, he also comments on what the staff as a whole has accomplished. As he gives each award, there is great applause. The staff feels good that its efforts are being recognized, and there is a strong feeling of camaraderie and community.

Celebrations shape and maintain the culture of the school and encourage progress toward the community objectives and toward the shared vision (DuFour & Eaker, 1998). Consistently honoring and celebrating positive actions sends an effective message of what is valued to old and new members of the school community. When you publicly honor and recognize behaviors that support the school vision, it is a powerful motivator that helps to maintain a positive school culture. Other important reasons to celebrate are (a) to engage in rituals and symbolism and recount stories that bind the members of the community together and (b) to impart the

---

Tips for Leaders 9.4

Tell a Story

When celebrating the accomplishment of individuals, tell a story about what they did, emphasizing how their behavior epitomizes the shared values of the community. Recount stories of past heroes and heroines as often as possible in celebrations and in informal situations.

---

values of the learning community to its members, its stakeholders, and the general public (Bolman & Deal, 1991, and Glickman, 2003).

Celebrations and School Improvement Efforts

Aside from shaping school culture, celebrations of success energize school improvement efforts. Saphier and King (1985, in Hirsh, 1996) document twelve norms of strong culture associated with school improvement. Among them are appreciation, recognition, and celebration. Indeed, celebrations are so important to maintaining school improvement efforts that the National Staff Development Council recommends that schools build celebrations into their action plans and assign duties to ensure that they are held (Hirsh, 1997).

It's fine to celebrate at the end of a project, but sometimes it takes a long time to complete an entire action plan and people might get discouraged along the way. Recognition of progress at certain benchmarks refreshes and energizes the staff to continue their efforts. Celebrations should be built into school improvement activities for the following purposes: (a) to measure progress and acknowledge reaching benchmarks, (b) to motivate team members to higher achievement, and (c) to keep community members focused on the action plan and the shared objectives (Glickman, 2003, Hirsh, 1997, Peterson & Deal, 1998).

The Role of Leaders

Leaders are not limited to the administrative ranks. Leaders may be staff members, parents, community members, or even students. Effective leaders articulate the shared values, identify and reinforce the positive aspects of the school culture, and try to change its negative factors (Peterson & Deal, 1998). They grasp all of the layers of the community's culture. Leaders understand the deepest layer, the values that undergird

---

Tips for Leaders 9.5

Strengthen the Norms

Have your staff collaboratively look at the cultural norms associated with effective schools. Have them give examples of each one in your learning community and discuss specific ways to strengthen them. See Saphier and King (1995, in Hirsh, 1996) for the norms and a process for doing this.

---

the community. Moreover, they engage in practices and build traditions that support these deeply held beliefs, thus operating at the second layer of culture. Finally, leaders are cognizant of the surface layer as well: They are very aware of the visible signs that help define and reinforce school culture, such as the motto on the school stationery or the trophies won by the math team on display in the lobby. Their words and deeds help mold the traditions, behaviors, and attitudes of the community.

As DuFour (1998) observes, effective leaders shape and maintain the culture in part through carefully selected celebrations. They recognize those who serve the organization's objectives. They recount stories of exemplary people who have worked to fulfill the school's vision. They publicly acknowledge the achievements of the staff and the students. They observe and celebrate benchmarks on the road to achievement. They keep the attention of the learning community on the students whom they serve. Moreover, through their own behaviors and demeanor, effective leaders model the beliefs that are the foundation of cultures (Deal & Peterson, 1990). In short, effective leaders are vigorous in identifying, celebrating, and modeling on an ongoing basis those behaviors and accomplishments that reinforce the positive aspects of the culture and that continually move the learning community closer to its vision.

Reasons to Celebrate

All actions or outcomes that promote the values of the learning community are reasons to celebrate. Behaviors and accomplishments of the staff, the students, or other community members that are aligned with the school's mission and vision are cause for accolades. Individual as well as group accomplishments should be recognized.

Individual recognition could be given to students' for academic achievement, to staff who make outstanding efforts in line with the values of the learning community, and to teachers who publish professional materials or get an advanced degree. Parents or community members who put forth extraordinary effort, such as school volunteers and those who serve as class parents, should also be recognized and celebrated.

Group achievements, such as classes with perfect attendance and academic or athletic team victories, should also be acknowledged. Another cause for celebration could be a committee reaching a benchmark in an action plan: You don't have to wait for the completion of the project. Businesses and universities who partner with schools should also be acknowledged and celebrated. All of these stakeholders make valuable contributions to the learning community and they deserve to be recognized. Recognition helps to sustain the commitment of all segments of the learning community.

Ways of Celebrating

Awards assemblies, plaques, dinners, teas, and other special events are traditional ways of celebrating success, but accomplishments may be recognized on an ongoing, day-by-day basis. Media coverage is a way of celebrating that lets the entire community become aware of the positive aspects of the learning community.

Celebrations do not have to always be formal events. They may occur within existing structures and formats. For example, if it is the practice within the school to make morning announcements, some of the successes may be announced at that time. Schools have come up with many creative ways of celebrating, some of which you may read about in Hirsh (1997).

Some Tips for Celebrations

A list of tips providing ideas for celebrating milestones in the learning community is provided below. The list includes ideas from Hirsh (1997), the National Staff Development Council ([NSDC] 1998), and our own knowledge base.

- Award progress toward a goal as well as the completion of a project. Acknowledgment of important benchmarks on the way to a goal is energizing.
- Include celebration times as action plan calendars are developed.
- Give awards that recipients will appreciate.
- At times, celebrate in ways that the general public can see or join. This keeps them informed and helps build support for the school.

- Celebrate mistakes sometimes. Teachers should not fear making mistakes. We can learn from our mistakes. Celebrating them sometimes encourages risk taking.

Collaboration

In order to maintain the learning community, it is important to provide ongoing support for cooperative efforts among the staff. Strategies for sustaining the structures that support a culture of collaboration are discussed in the next section.

HOW DO WE SUSTAIN THE STRUCTURES THAT SUPPORT LEARNING COMMUNITY SCHOOLS?

As we have discussed in earlier chapters, learning community schools are supported by a variety of structured activities that allow teachers and other staff members to come together to share ideas, to observe one another teaching, to learn new strategies, and to make plans for improving teaching and learning. Schools require many different kinds of structured learning opportunities to meet the diverse learning needs, interests, and styles of teachers, staff, and students. It is important that teachers be cognizant of the purpose and value of ongoing participation in these activities, as their participation generates new learning that nurtures and sustains the learning community.

Those in leadership positions must, therefore, take steps to ensure that teachers have multiple learning opportunities and are empowered to act upon what they have learned. A set of tips that leaders can use to maintain the structures that support ongoing learning is provided below. These ideas are expressed earlier throughout the text.

- Provide teachers with training in the group process skills needed to effectively participate in teams and committees. New staff members should get training in order to acculturate them and bring them up to speed. Advanced training may be offered to those who have had the basics in conflict management.

- Ensure that teachers are provided with the time needed for conversation and group reflection around instructional issues in regularly scheduled grade-level meetings, content area meetings, team meetings, study groups, and/or professional development activities.

- Structure and adhere to a schedule that affords all teachers the opportunity to observe each other's teaching.

Tips for Leaders 9.6

Spread the Word

Principals can support and sustain such structures as teams, committees, and study groups by publicly acknowledging the outcomes of their work on a regularly scheduled basis in newsletters and faculty meetings. It is through communication that expectations for the outcomes of teamwork are established and sustained.

- Providing concentrated content-based instructional support for teachers over time helps to sustain the learning community. For example, in the Plainfield, New Jersey, school district, a teacher is identified in each elementary school that has expertise in literacy instruction. Fifty percent of the support teacher's time is scheduled to provide support in literacy instruction for the other teachers in the school. Now that student achievement in literacy has improved significantly over the past five years, the district will move on to structure in-depth instructional support in mathematics.

- Demonstrate the importance of structured activities through regular visits to team and committee meetings. Keep in mind, however, that these meetings are structured to be teacher led and that their decisions should be honored.

WHAT MUST WE DO TO MAINTAIN THE FOCUS ON CONTINUOUS STUDENT LEARNING THAT CHARACTERIZES LEARNING COMMUNITIES?

One of the characteristics of a learning community is the focus on continuous student learning. Several factors help maintain this focus, such as ongoing data collection, looking at student work, and professional development.

Ongoing Data Collection and Analysis

Continuous examination of data, especially student data, is important for sustaining the professional learning community (Bernhardt, 1998; Holcomb, 1999; Johnson, 2002). In order to monitor and sustain school improvement, procedures have to be put in place for regular monitoring of student performance throughout the year, most intensively in those areas in which the greatest improvement is sought. Data should be collected throughout the year on a regular basis, not just at the end of the year. Data may also be collected from end-of-chapter tests. Many schools collect data on a quarterly basis. Bernhardt (1998), Richardson (2000), and Schmoker (2001) provide many other examples of how schools may collect and analyze data on an ongoing basis for the purpose of school improvement.

The Role of Teachers

Formulative data and summative data should be looked at by both supervisors and teachers, not just supervisors alone. It is important in the learning community that data be in the hands of teachers. Teachers can then have conversations about teaching and learning based on the data and make informed decisions about changing their practice. Teachers have many reasons for avoiding the analysis of data. Holcomb (1999) points out that they may lack the time or the training, or they may think that the results will be used to evaluate them, especially in this era of high-stakes testing. It is important that teachers be provided with training in this area.

The Role of Leadership

As in the examples mentioned above, the principal and other leaders should take an active part in collecting and examining data throughout the school year. The leader should ensure that the data get into the hands of the teachers and that they analyze and synthesize them, and discuss the implications for classroom instruction on an ongoing basis.

Furthermore, leaders—from central office staff to principals, from supervisors to team leaders—should all be asking the right questions and monitoring activities surrounding data collection and assessment at administrative meetings and faculty meetings (Schmoker, 2001). Examples of such questions follow: *Are all of the teachers aware at all times of their school improvement goals? What evidence is there that they are working effectively toward these goals? What effective strategies have been developed to correct the identified academic shortcomings?*

Equity

A learning community dedicated to equity ensures that all students achieve, regardless of race, culture, ethnicity, or gender. Therefore, student data should be disaggregated so that the staff may see how various groups of students are achieving and make adjustments in strategies and resources as needed to ensure equitable outcomes. Ongoing data-driven

---

Tips for Leaders 9.7

Analyze for Equity

When analyzing disaggregated data, have your teachers discuss and reflect on such questions as these:

- What patterns in achievement do we see in the data across the groups?
- Which teaching strategies worked best for selected groups of students?
- How did specific teaching strategies or programs affect student academic outcomes?
- Which groups of students made improvements?
- What strategies do teachers use with their students to address the standards?
- What does the data tell us about our professional development needs regarding equity?
- Are all groups meeting the district content standards?

---

decision making is imperative for maintaining the focus on student learning. Johnson (2002) provides comprehensive strategies and tools for collecting, analyzing, and applying data for greater equity in student performance. We also recommend that groups who are concerned with equity use the series of questions posed in Tips for Leaders 9.7 to analyze data after they have been disaggregated.

Student Input

In addition to performance data, student input should be included as a source of data, particularly at the secondary level. High-school students, an often-neglected source of information, should be encouraged to participate on decision-making committees, focus groups, and surveys, where appropriate.

Looking at Student Work

Collaborative examination of student work, by definition, keeps the focus on student learning. This should be done on an ongoing basis, zeroing in on areas of student performance that need strengthening in accord with the annual objectives. As previously discussed, the collaborative assessment of student work should inform instruction. In sustaining the focus on continuous student learning, principals also get involved in examining work samples.

For example, in one New Jersey school, one of the objectives is to increase the ability of fourth grade students to do open-ended problem solving in mathematics, so the principal collects work samples from all of the fourth grade classes every week. Together, the teachers and the principal look at the students' work and make adjustments in instruction accordingly. They do not wait until the end of the year for the standardized scores to come back. As another example, in a school in New York City with a focus on improving writing, the principal collects writing samples from a different class every Monday. The principal then visits the class during the week to share with the students her reflections on and pleasure in the student work. She sometimes discusses writing with an individual child. This sustains the children's interest in their work and keeps the teachers focused on student performance.

Professional Development

Professional development in the learning community has improved student performance as its ultimate goal. In order to sustain the focus on student learning, professional development must be job embedded and directly related to information gained from student performance. Some strategies previously discussed are summarized below.

- The thrust of professional development for the learning community should be readdressed annually by the staff. Individual teachers should also assess their own professional growth on an annual basis and make plans each year for improving their practice with the ultimate aim of strengthening student learning.

- Professional portfolios should be updated on a continuous basis. Teachers should assess their portfolios annually and plan their personal professional development activities accordingly. This may be done individually and in small groups to promote collaborative learning among teachers.

- Special programs of professional development, orientation, and mentorship should be provided to new teachers to orientate them to the culture and practices of the learning community.

- Assess the professional development program on an ongoing basis using multiple sources of data. Make adjustments to the program accordingly.

HOW DO WE MAINTAIN A FOCUS ON THE SCHOOL'S MISSION AND SHARED VISION STATEMENTS THAT STRESS STUDENT ACHIEVEMENT?

The importance of mission and vision statements around which members of a learning community can focus their energy has been emphasized through this book. A school with learning community characteristics can be energized by clear and specific mission statements that focus on academic success. The Evergreen School and the Hugo Newman College Preparatory School, which were discussed in earlier chapters, are two examples of such schools.

Accordingly, efforts should be made to highlight and provide ongoing reminders of the mission and vision to the school community. Schools use a variety of strategies to accomplish this. In one high school, the principal takes the staff on a retreat at the beginning of the year to sharpen their focus on the school's mission and vision and to set specific goals for the upcoming school year. In another school, the principal, staff, and student representatives develop a new motto each school year that is in line with their mission. This motto is publicized throughout the school community and is posted prominently across the school campus.

In working with schools, we have found that it is essential for schools in the process of change to monitor the extent to which they are making progress towards achieving their vision and meeting their goals. It is critical for schools to continually measure the effectiveness of the strategies selected for building the learning community. Our experience with schools has led us to conclude that it is to the schools' benefit to establish a formal ongoing process for assessing progress toward change. One model for this purpose is the Critical Friends Group (CFG), a program that was initially developed by the Coalition of Essential Schools (1999). It can be used as an ongoing, collaborative self-analysis process for sustaining the learning community.

Using Critical Friends Groups to Sustain Community

A CFG is composed of a group of teachers in a school who meet monthly to explore their instructional practices and improve student achievement. Guided by a skilled coach, the group uses a set of structured collegial dialogues, known as *protocols*, to take a careful look at a school's curriculum and teaching practices, to explore a school's culture as it relates to student outcomes, or to identify goals and set priorities.

Information Online 9.1

Read the article *Critical Friends*, by Deborah Bambino, available at http://www.ascd.org/readingroom/edlead/ 0203/bambino. html, for specific examples of how the CFG process and protocols have been used to help teachers improve instruction and student learning.

Instructional or organizational practices and standards may be changed based on what has been learned during the process. Additional detailed information about the CFG process can be found at the Website listed in Information Online 9.1.

The CFG protocols are structured to maximize the potential for group meetings to be productive. Each protocol has guidelines for the roles to be played by the coach and other participants in the CFG. Authentic examples of how CFGs have been used to aid teachers in improving teaching and learning can be found at the Website listed in Information Online 9.2.

The CFG Process and the Learning Community Characteristics

- The CFG process is characterized by a set of features that contribute to the sustaining of community and maintaining a focus on the school's mission and vision. The process provides a long-term, structured process with student achievement and community building as its most important goals. These goals are aligned with the mission and vision of the learning community.

- The process provides for the ongoing professional growth of teachers. The participating teachers are committed to working together for a period of over two years.

- Teachers learn to consistently engage in collaborative behaviors and become skilled in reflecting on their own teaching practices and those of their colleagues.

- Most importantly, because the CFGs meet over a long period of time, they can become a productive way of assessing a school's progress toward instructional change and progress toward achieving the school's vision.

Information Online 9.2

To learn about the Critical Friends Group (CFG) process, visit the Critical Friends Website at http:// cesnorthwest.org/critical_friends_groups.htm. Extensive information is provided about the expectations, goals, and expected outcomes for CFG members, CFG coaches, principals, and students. Additionally, descriptions of the protocols, helpful hints, guiding questions, and detailed steps on conducting the protocols are included in this site.

WHAT STEPS MUST BE TAKEN TO ENSURE THAT SHARED LEADERSHIP IS SUSTAINED IN LEARNING COMMUNITY SCHOOLS?

Developing and maintaining shared leadership is central to sustaining the learning community. It is also important to keep a balance between the practice of shared leadership and the use of formal leadership. Some areas to consider in sustaining shared leadership in the learning community are suggested below.

Developing New Leaders

It is important to continuously develop new leaders in order to sustain the learning community. Some ways of doing this are to

- Make certain that new teachers are acculturated into the concepts and practices of shared leadership.
- Rotate leadership within teams so that as many staff members as possible have the opportunity for leadership.
- Publicly acknowledge teachers who voluntarily take on leadership roles.
- Use the talents of teachers for schoolwide professional development activities.

Ongoing Leadership Training

It is important to provide leadership training opportunities for all of the staff. Beyond that, principals must make sure that teacher-leaders develop expertise in such areas as data collection and analysis and that they have knowledge of educational research and specialized sources of curricular pedagogical support.

The Principal's Role

Principals contribute to the long-term maintenance of the learning community by building teacher leadership throughout the staff and nurturing shared leadership. It is important for those in leadership positions to participate in professional development activities and other change related activities that are part of the reform efforts. The principal's involvement indicates that engagement in learning activities is an important part of what occurs in the school and provides a model of leadership for others to follow.

CONCLUSION

It takes at least as much thought and effort to sustain a professional learning community as it does to create it. If we want to have a long-lasting, positive impact on student achievement, then we must think about maintenance even as we plan school reform. There must be ongoing, daily attention to the elements that support the learning community: a focus on student outcomes, collaborative learning, shared leadership, and commitment to a common vision. The importance of establishing processes to sustain learning opportunities for members of the school community cannot be overemphasized.

We hope that this book has provided a guide to get you started on your own journey toward your vision of a learning community.

ACTIVITIES

1. Working with colleagues, identify the rituals, symbols, and stories in your school culture. Discuss what shared values they represent. Are there any that do not truly mirror your current shared values and that should be discarded? Are there any values that exist in your learning community that are not addressed in your rituals, symbols, and stories?

2. Read the articles about CFGs listed in Information Online 9.1 and 9.2. Then,

   a. Provide a group of interested teachers with an awareness session on the CFG Process.

   b. Select an appropriate CFG protocol and use it with the teachers to examine student work samples, provide feedback to a teacher, examine and discuss professional literature, or explore some other area that is of interest to the participating teachers.

   c. Close the session by allowing the group to use questions such as those listed below to reflect on the protocol.

      • What new knowledge did they acquire?

      • What are the benefits of using the protocol?

      • Would this protocol be useful for some of the group activities in our school?

      • How could the process be improved?

   d. Make plans for follow-up sessions using the protocols.

3. Using this chapter as a starting point, identify the strategies that your school uses to sustain itself as a learning community.

References

Acheson, K. A., & Gall, M. D. (1997). *Techniques in the clinical supervision of teachers.* New York: Longman. Available online at http://www.yk.psu.edu/~jlg18/495/critical_friends1.pdf.

Ancess, J. (2000). The reciprocal influence of teacher learning, teaching practice, school restructuring, and student learning outcomes. *Teacher College Record, 102*(3), 590–619.

Annenburg Institute for School Reform. (2001). Looking at Student Work [Website]. Retrieved March 14, 2003, from http://lasw.org/welcome.html.

Bambino, D. (2002). Critical friends. *Educational Leadership, 59*(6), 25–27. Retrieved March 30, 2003, from http://www.ascd.org/readingroom/edlead/0203/bambino.html.

Barlow, V. E. (2001, June). *Trust and the principalship.* Retrieved December 21, 2002, from http://www.ucalgary.co/~cll/resources/trustandtheprincipalship.pdf.

Barnes, F., Miller, M., & Dennis, R. (2001). Face to face. *Journal of Staff Development, 22*(4). Retrieved March 30, 2003, from http://www.nsdc.org/library/jsd/barnes224.html.

Barth, R. S. (1990). *Improving schools from within.* San Francisco: Jossey-Bass.

Bennis, W. G., & Nanus, B. (1986). *Leaders: Strategies for taking charge.* New York: Harper & Row.

Bernhardt, V. L. (1998). *Data analysis for comprehensive schoolwide improvement.* Larchmont, NY: Eye on Education.

Birchak, B., Connor, C., Crawford, K., Kahn, L., Kaser, S., Turner, S., & Short, K. (1998). *Teacher study groups: Building community through dialogue and reflection.* Urbana, IL: National Council of Teachers of English.

Birman, B. F., Desimone, L., Porter, A. C., & Garet, M. S. (2000). Designing professional development that works. *Educational Leadership, 57*(8), 28–32.

Blase, J., & Blase, J. (1999). Principals' instructional leadership and teacher development: Teachers' perspectives. *Educational Administration Quarterly, 35*(3), 349–378.

Bolman, L. G., & Deal, T. E. (1991). *Reframing organizations: Artistry, choice and leadership.* San Francisco: Jossey-Bass.

Bonstigl, J. J. (2001). *Schools of quality: An introduction to total quality management in education* (3rd ed.). Thousand Oaks, CA: Corwin.

Bryk, A. S., & Schneider, B. (2002). *Trust in schools: A core resource for improvement.* New York: Russell Sage.

Bull, B., & Buechler, M. (1996). *Learning together: Professional development for better schools.* Bloomington, IN: Indiana Education Policy Center for the Indiana Department of Education.

Bullock, A. A., & Hawk, P. P. (2001). *Developing a teaching portfolio: A guide for pre-service and practicing teacher.* Upper Saddle River, NJ: Prentice Hall.

Campbell, D. M., Cignetti, P. B., Melenyzer, B. J., Nettles, D. H., & Wyman, R. M. (2001). *How to develop a professional portfolio: A manual for teachers* (2nd ed.). Boston: Allyn & Bacon.

Carr, J. F., & Harris, D. E. (2001). *Succeeding with standards: Linking curriculum, assessment, and action planning.* Alexandria, VA: Association for Supervision and Curriculum Development.

Chance, E. W., & Grady, M. L. (1990, November). Creating and implementing a vision for the school. *NASSP Bulletin 74*(529), 12–18. (Eric Document Reproduction Service No. EJ 418 117).

Charles A. Dana Center, University of Texas at Austin. (1999). *Hope for urban education: A study of nine high-performing, high-poverty, urban elementary schools.* Washington, DC: U.S. Department of Education, Planning and Evaluation Service.

Coalition of Essential Schools. (1999). Critical friends groups. Retrieved November 24, 2002, from http://cesnorthwest.org/critical_friends_ groups. htm.

Cogan, M. L. (1973). *Clinical supervision.* Boston: Houghton Mifflin.

Collay, M., Dunlap, D., Enloe, W., & Gagnon, G. W. (1998). *Learning circles.* Thousand Oaks, CA: Corwin.

Conley, D., Dunlap, D., & Goldman, P. (1992, Winter). The "vision thing" and school restructuring. *OSSC Report 32*(2), 1–8. (Eric Document Reproduction Service No. ED 343 246).

Conley, D., & Goldman, P. (1994). Ten propositions for facilitative leadership. In J. Murphy & K. S. Louis (Eds.), *Reshaping the principalship* (pp. 237–262). Thousand Oaks, CA: Corwin.

Cramer, G., Hurst, B., & Wilson, C. (1996). *Teacher study groups for professional development* (Fastback 406). Bloomington, IN: Phi Delta Kappa.

Crow, G. M., & Matthews, L. J. (1998). *Finding one's way: How mentoring can lead to dynamic leadership.* Thousand Oaks, CA: Corwin.

Cushman, K. (1996). Looking collaboratively at student work: An essential toolkit. *Horace, 13*(2), 1–12. Retrieved March 30, 2003, from http://www.essentials schools.org/cs/resources/view/ces_res/57.

Daresh, C. J., & Playko, M. A. (1995). *Supervision as a proactive process: Concepts and cases* (2nd ed.). Prospect Heights, IL: Waveland.

Deal, T. E., & Peterson, K. D. (1990). *The principal's role in shaping school culture.* Alexandria, VA: U. S. Department of Education and National Association of Elementary Principals, Office of Educational Research and Improvement. Reprinted March 1991 by the National Association of Elementary School Principals [NAESP].

Deal, T. E., & Peterson, K. D. (1994). *The leadership paradox: Balancing logic and artistry in schools.* San Francisco: Jossey-Bass.

Denmark, V. M., & Podsen, I. J. (2000). The mettle of a mentor: What it takes to make this relationship work for all. *Journal of Staff Development, 21*(4), 19–23.

Deutsch, M. (1973). *The resolution of conflict: Constructive and destructive process.* New Haven: Yale University Press.

Dickman, M. H., & Stanford-Blair, N. (2002). *Connecting leadership to the brain.* Thousand Oaks, CA: Corwin.

DuFour, R. (1998). Why celebrate? It sends a vivid message about what is valued. *Journal of Staff Development, 19*(4). Retrieved March 22, 2003, from http://www.nsdc.org/library/jsd/dufour194.html.

DuFour, R., & Eaker, R. (1998). *Professional learning communities at work: Best practices for enhancing student achievement.* Reston, VA: Association for Supervision and Curriculum Development.

Elliot, V., & Schiff, S. (2001). Staff developers use structures, inquiry, and reflection to examine feelings about equity. *Journal of Staff Development, 22*(2). Retrieved March 30, 2003, from http://www.nsdc.org/library/jsd/elliott222.html.

Elmore, R. F., Peterson, P. L., & McCarthey, S. J. (1996). *Restructuring in the classroom: Teaching, learning, and school organization.* San Francisco: Jossey-Bass.

Fisher, B. (1998). *Joyful learning in kindergarten.* Portsmouth, NH: Heinemann.

Fisher, R., & Brown, S. (1988). *Getting together: Building a relationship that gets to yes.* Boston: Houghton Mifflin.

Fisher, R., & Ury, W. (1981). *Getting to yes: Negotiating agreement without giving in.* Harrisonburg, VA: R. R. Donnelley.

Fullan, M. (with Stiegelbauer, S.). (1991). *The new meaning of educational change.* New York: Teachers College Press.

Fullan, M. (1993). *Change forces: Probing the depths of educational reform.* London: Falmer.

Ganser, T. (2001). New teacher mentor. *Journal of Staff Development, 22*(1), 39–41.

Glacel, B. P., & Robert, E. A., Jr. (1994). *Light bulbs for leaders: A guidebook for leaders and teams.* Burke, VA: Vima International.

Glickman, C. D. (2003). Symbols and celebrations that sustain education. *Educational Leadership, 60*(6), 34–39.

Goldhammer, R. (1969). *Clinical supervision: Special methods for the supervision of teachers.* New York: Holt, Rinehart, and Winston.

Goldhammer, R., Anderson, R. H., & Krajewski, R. J. (1993). *Clinical supervision: Special methods for the supervision of teachers* (3rd ed.). San Diego: Harcourt Brace Jovanovich.

Guskey, T. R. (2000). *Evaluating professional development.* Thousand Oaks, CA: Corwin.

Guskey, T. R. (2002). Does it make a difference? Evaluating professional development. *Educational Leadership, 59*(6), 45–51.

Hackman, J. R. (1990). *Groups that work and those that don't.* San Francisco: Jossey-Bass.

Hall, G. E., & Hord, S. M. (2001). *Implementing change: Patterns, principles and potholes.* Boston: Allyn & Bacon.

Hallinger, P., & Heck, R. (1996). Reassessing the principal's role in school effectiveness: A review of empirical research, 1980–1995. *Educational Administration Quarterly, 32*(1), 5–44.

Harrington-Mackin, D. (1994). *The team building tool kit: Tips, tactics and rules for effective workplace teams.* New York: AMACOM.

Hirsh, S. (1996, October). Creating a healthy school culture is everyone's business. *School Team Innovator.* Retrieved May 29, 2002, from http://www.nsdc.org/library/innovator/inn10-96hirsh.html.

Hirsh, S. (1997, April). Keeping your school improvement plan on track. *School Team Innovator.* Retrieved May 2, 2002, from http://www.nsdc.org/library/innovator/inn4-97hirsh.html.

Hoffman, J. D., Sabo, D., Bliss, J., & Hoy, W. (1994). Building a culture of trust. *Journal of School Leadership, 4*(5), 484–502.

Holcomb, E. L. (1999). *Getting excited about data: How to combine people, passion and proof.* Thousand Oaks, CA: Corwin.

Hord, S. M. (1997). *Professional learning communities: Communities of continuous inquiry and improvement.* Austin, TX: Southwest Educational Development Laboratory.

Hudson, J. S. (2002). Friday forums. *Educational Leadership, 59*(6), 76–77.

Institute of Learning. (1998). *The Learning Walk*sm. Pittsburgh: University of Pittsburgh, Institute for Learning. Retrieved December 12, 2002, from http://www.instituteforlearning.org/ifl.html.

Interstate New Teacher Assessment and Support Consortium. (1992). *Model standards for beginning teacher licensing, assessment and development: A resource for state dialogue.* Washington, DC: Council of Chief State School Officers.

Interstate School Leaders Licensure Consortium. (1996). *Standards for school leaders.* Washington, DC: Council of Chief State School Officers.

Irby, B. J., & Brown, G. (2000). *The career advancement portfolios.* Thousand Oaks, CA: Corwin.

Jacobs, H. H. (1997). *Mapping the big picture: Integrating curriculum and assessment K–12.* Alexandria, VA: Association for Supervision and Curriculum Development.

Jensen, E. (1998). *Teaching with the brain in mind.* Alexandria, VA: Association for Supervision and Curriculum Development.

Johnson, D. W., & Johnson, F. P. (2000). *Joining together: Group theory and group skills* (7th ed.). Boston: Allyn & Bacon.

Johnson, R. S. (2002). *Using data to close the achievement gap: How to measure equity in our schools.* Thousand Oaks, CA: Corwin.

Joyce, B., & Showers, B. (1988). *Student achievement through staff development.* New York: Longman.

Katzenbach, J. R., & Smith, D. K. (1993). *The wisdom of teams: Creating the high performance organization.* Boston: Harvard Business School Press.

Knowles, M., Holton, E., & Swanson, R. A. (1998). *The adult learner.* Newton, MA: Butterworth-Heinemann.

Kruse, S. D., Louis, K. S., & Bryk, A. (1995). An emerging framework for analyzing school-based professional community. In K. S. Louis & S. D. Kruse (Eds.), *Professionalism and Community: Perspectives on Reforming Urban Schools* (pp. 23–42). Thousand Oaks, CA: Corwin.

Lambert, L. (1998). *Building leadership capacity in schools.* Alexandria, VA: Association for Supervision and Curriculum Development.

Lambert, L., Walker, D., Zimmerman, D. P., Cooper, J. E., Lambert, M. D., Gardner, M. E., & Ford-Slack, P. J. (1995). *The constructivist leader.* New York: Teachers College Press.

Lashway, L. (1997). *Leading with vision.* Eugene, OR: ERIC Clearinghouse on Educational Management.

Lewis, A. (1997). A new consensus emerges on the characteristics of good professional development. *The Harvard Letter, 13*(3), 3.

Little, J. W. (1990). The persistence of privacy: Autonomy and initiative in teachers' professional relations. *Teachers College Record, 91,* 509–536.

Louis, K. S., & Kruse, S. D. (1995). *Professionalism and community: Perspectives on reforming urban schools.* Thousand Oaks, CA: Corwin.

Louis, K. S., Marks, H. M., & Kruse, S. D. (1996). Teachers' professional community in restructuring schools. *American Educational Research Journal, 33*(4), 757–798.

Martin-Kniep, G. O. (1999). *Capturing the wisdom of practice.* Alexandria, VA: Association for Supervision and Curriculum Development.

McEwan, E. K. (1998). *Seven steps to effective instructional leadership.* Thousand Oaks, CA: Corwin.

Mitchell, G. (1998). *The trainers handbook: The AMA guide to effective training* (3rd ed.). New York: AMACOM.

Mohr, N. (1998). Creating effective study groups for principals. *Educational Leadership, 55*(7), 41–44.

Mullins, T. W. (1994). *Staff development programs: A guide to evaluation.* Thousand Oaks, CA: Corwin.

Murphy, C., & Lick, D. (2001). *Whole faculty study groups: Creating student based staff development* (2nd ed.). Thousand Oaks, CA: Corwin.

Myers, C. B., & Simpson, D. J. (1998). *Re-creating schools: Places where everyone learns and likes it.* Thousand Oaks, CA: Corwin.

National PTA. (1998). *National standards for parent/family involvement programs.* Retrieved November 30, 2002, from http://www.pta.org/parentinvolvement/standards/pfistand.asp.

National Staff Development Council. (1998, April–May). Applause! Applause! *Tools for Schools.* Retrieved May 2, 2002, from http://www.nsdc.org/ library/ tools/4-98lead.html.

National Staff Development Council. (2001). *By your own design: A teacher's professional learning guide* [CD ROM]. Oxford, OH: Author.

Nieto, S. M. (2002). Profoundly multicultural questions. *Educational Leadership, 60*(4), 6–10.

Noe, L. R. (2002). Heard the one about the principal who painted the door? *Journal of Staff Development, 23*(3), 20–22.

Northeast and Islands Regional Educational Laboratory at Brown University, the National School Network, & the Teacher Enhancement Electronic Communications Hall. (1999). *Electronic Collaboration: A Practical Guide for Educators.* Providence, RI: The LAB at Brown University.

Osterman, K. F. (1993). *Communication skills: A key to caring, collaboration, and change.* A paper presented at the annual conference of the University Council for Educational Administration, Houston, Texas, October 29–31, 1993. (Eric Document Reproduction Service No. ED 363 973).

Owens, R. G. (2001). *Organizational behavior in education: Instructional leadership and school reform* (7th ed.). Boston: Allyn & Bacon.

Painter, B. (2001). Using teaching portfolios. *Educational Leadership, 58*(2), 31–34.

Peterson, K. D., & Deal, T. E. (1998). How leaders influence the culture of schools. *Educational Leadership, 56*(1), 28–30.

Plunkett, W. R. (1995). *Supervision: Diversity and teams in the workplace* (8th ed.). Upper Saddle River, NJ: Prentice Hall.

Pokorny, N. (1997). *Leading the Charge for Change.* Denver, CO: RMC Research Corporation. Retrieved November 27, 2002, from http://www.starcenter.org/ products/articles/change.html.

Portner, H. (1998). *Mentoring new teachers.* Thousand Oaks, CA: Corwin.

Powers, D., Thompson, S., & Buckner, K. (2001). Electronic portfolios. In A. A. Bullock & P. P. Hawk (Eds.), *Developing a teaching portfolio: A guide for pre-service and practicing teachers* (pp. 123–134). Upper Saddle River, NJ: Prentice Hall.

Pruitt, D. G., & Rubin, J. Z. (1986). *Social conflict: Escalation, stalemate and settlement.* New York: Random House.

Purkey, S. C., & Smith, M. S. (1983). Effective schools: A review. *The Elementary School Journal, 83*(4), 427–452.

Richardson, J. (2000, August–September,). Smart moves: Achieving your vision depends on follow through. *Tools for Schools.* Retrieved May 2, 2002, from http://www.nsdc.org/library/tools/tools9-00rich.html.

Richardson, J. (2001a, February). Student work at the core of teacher learning. *Results,* 1–6.

Richardson, J. (2001b, February–March). Group wise strategies for examining student work together. *Tools for Schools,* 1–2.

Richardson, J. (2001c, March). Team learning: Teachers who learn together improve together. *Results,* 1–6.

Richardson, J. (2002, February–March). Reach for the stars. *Tools for Schools,* 1–6.

Robbins, H., & Finley, M. (1995). *Why teams don't work: What went wrong and how to make it right.* Princeton, NJ: Peterson's Pacesetter.

Roberts, M. P. (2001). *Your mentor: A practical guide for first-year teachers in Grades 1–3.* Thousand Oaks, CA: Corwin.

Rodgers, C. (2002). Seeing student learning: Teacher change, and the role of reflection. *Harvard Educational Review, 72*(2), 230–253.

Saphier, J., & King, M. (1985, March). Good seeds grow in strong culture. *Educational Leadership,* 67–74.

Sarason, S. B. (1990). *The predictable failure of school reform.* San Francisco: Jossey-Bass.

Schmoker, M. (2001). *The results fieldbook: Practical strategies from dramatically improved schools.* Alexandria, VA: Association for Supervision and Curriculum Development.

Schmuck, R. A., & Runkel, P. J. (1994). *The handbook of organization development in schools and colleges* (4th ed.). Prospect Heights, IL: Waveland.

Senge, P. (1990). *The fifth discipline: The art and practice of the learning organization.* New York: Doubleday.

Senge, P. (1994). *The fifth discipline fieldbook: Strategies and tools for building a learning organization.* New York: Doubleday.

Senge, P., Cambron-McCabe, N., Lucas, T., Smith, B., Dutton, J., & Kleiner, A. (2000). *Schools that learn.* New York: Doubleday.

Sergiovanni, T. J. (1992). *Moral leadership: Getting to the heart of school improvement.* San Franciso: Jossey-Bass.

Sergiovanni, T. J. (2001). *The principalship: A reflective practice perspective.* Boston: Allyn & Bacon.

Shore, R. (1997). *Rethinking the brain: New insights into early development.* New York: Families and Work Institute.

Smit, G. M. (2001, December). To infuse new thinking, try book discussions. *School Administrator* [Web Edition]. Retrieved February 22, 2003, from http://www.aasa.org/publications/sa/2001_12/focus_smit.htm.

Smith, C. S., & Piele, P. K. (Eds.). (1997). *School leadership handbook for excellence.* Eugene, OR: University of Oregon, ERIC Clearinghouse on Educational Management.

Smith, M. K. (2001). Peter Senge and the learning organization. *The encyclopedia of informal education.* Retrieved March 29, 2003, from http://www.infed.org/thinkers/senge.htm.

Sousa, D. A. (2001a). *How the brain learns* (2nd ed.). Thousand Oaks, CA: Corwin.

Sousa, D. A. (2001b). *How the special needs brain learns.* Thousand Oaks, CA: Corwin.

Sousa, D. A. (2002). *How the gifted brain learns.* Thousand Oaks, CA: Corwin.

Sparks, D. (1993, November). Thirteen tips for managing change. *Wisconsin School News.* Retrieved March 29, 2003, from http://www.ncrel.org/sdrs/areas/issues/educatrs/leadrshp/le5spark.htm.

Sparks, D., & Hirsh, S. (1997). *A new vision for staff development.* Alexandria, VA: Association for Supervision and Curriculum Development.

Speck, M. (1999). *The principalship: Building a learning community.* Upper Saddle River, NJ: Prentice Hall.

Starratt, R. J. (1995). *Leaders with vision: The quest for school renewal.* Thousand Oaks, CA: Corwin.

Sullivan, S., & Glanz, J. (2000). *Supervision that improves instruction.* Thousand Oaks, CA: Corwin.

Trumbell, E., Rothstein-Fisch, C., & Greenfield, P. M. (2001). Cultural views of collectivism and individualism come into play in school. *Journal of Staff Development, 22*(2), 10–14.

Tschannen-Moran, M., & Hoy, W. K. (1998). Trust in schools: A conceptual and empirical analysis. *Journal of Educational Administration, 36*(4), 334–352.

Tuckman, B. W. (1965). Development sequence in small groups. *Psychological Bulletin, 63*(6), 384–399.

Van Wagenen, L., & Hibbard, K. M. (1998). Building teacher portfolios. *Educational Leadership, 55*(5), 26–29.

Wald, P. J., & Castleberry, M. S. (2000). *Educators as learners: Creating a professional learning community in your school.* Alexandria, VA: Association for Supervision and Curriculum Development.

Wallace, R. C., Engel, D. E., & Mooney, J. E. (1997). *The learning school, a guide to vision-based leadership.* Thousand Oaks, CA: Corwin.

Whitaker, K. S., & Moses, M. C. (1994). The restructuring handbook: A guide to school revitalization. Boston: Allyn & Bacon.

Wilhelm, J. D. (2001). *Improving comprehension with think-aloud strategies.* New York: Scholastic.

Williams, L. R., & De Gaetano, Y. (1985). *ALERTA: A multicultural, bilingual approach to teaching young children.* Reading, MA: Addison-Wesley.

Wolf, K. (1996). Developing an effective teaching portfolio. *Educational Leadership, 53*(6), 34–39.

Wolfe, P. (2001). *Brain matters: Translating research into classroom practice.* Alexandria, VA: Association for Supervision and Curriculum Development.

Wood, F. H., & McQuarrie, F. (1999). On-the -job-learning. *Journal of Staff Development, 20*(3), 10–13.

Wyatt, R. L., III, & Looper, S. (1999). *So you have to have a portfolio: A teacher's guide to preparation and presentation.* Thousand Oaks, CA: Corwin.

York-Barr, J., Sommers, W. A., Ghere, G. S., & Montie, J. (Eds.). (2001). *Reflective practice to improve schools: An action guide for educators.* Thousand Oaks, CA: Corwin.

Index

**CORWIN
PRESS**

The Corwin Press logo—a raven striding across an open book—represents the happy union of courage and learning. We are a professional-level publisher of books and journals for K-12 educators, and we are committed to creating and providing resources that embody these qualities. Corwin's motto is "Success for All Learners."